The Strength of a Woman

Unveiling Unparalleled Resilience and Power of Women through the Ages

Dr. Mimi Nkwepo

ISBN 979-8-89526-113-2 (paperback)
ISBN 979-8-89526-114-9 (digital)

Christian Faith Publishing
832 Park Avenue
Meadville, PA 16335
www.christianfaithpublishing.com

Printed in the United States of America

CONTENTS

INTRODUCTION

*Resilient women rise from the ashes of
adversity; their strength is an unbreakable
shield against the storms of life, inspiring others
with their courage and determination.*

Every woman has a story worth telling, regardless of her background or experiences. Some women have faced incredible challenges and overcome them while others have encountered difficult situations that have left them feeling hurt and vulnerable. Nonetheless, each woman's story holds significant importance in shaping the next generation of women. Women face numerous disparities daily, which are not always limited to their personal lives but often extend to their social, professional, academic, or even financial spheres.

In a world where women continuously face some of the worst challenges, it is crucial to advocate for opportunities that empower women to rise above these circumstances. Growing up in Africa, where patriarchal systems prevail, I would frequently question the value I could ever bring to the world. Of course, it can seem limiting to dream beyond what is presented within your immediate environment, but I have always challenged myself by asking, "Who said I couldn't have it all?"

Having moved to the United Kingdom at a very young age, I knew early on that I was destined to be a catalyst for positive change, not only in my life but also in the lives of those around me. My roles as a mother, wife, and doctor may be central to my identity, but I have also become a source of inspiration for young girls and women by motivating them to stay optimistic about their futures.

We all know how women breaking barriers or sexist conformities are often shunned because of the "threat" this seemingly poses in a predominantly male-orientated society. I surpassed these by starting my journey in hospitality management, then human resources and talent acquisition. This was when my passion for helping others became most apparent, motivating me to pursue my master's in human resource management and further my studies by obtaining a doctor of business administration in human resource management. This is quite exemplary of how setting your mind to something means that it is already achievable, and while it may look like I might have it all together, there certainly are days when I need to take a step back and recenter my focus on my well-being.

As a loving mother to two amazing sons and a compassionate wife, I still find myself juggling multiple responsibilities, including my role as the National Head of Talent Acquisition at Coach USA chairing the Thomas Edison University School of Management Dean's advisory board, in addition to my entrepreneurial ventures. All these roles each demand a certain level of my attention, but one thing I never grow weary of while performing any of them is my unwavering positivity and ensuring that it always reaches wherever it needs to.

Now you may be wondering what the relevance of sharing all this information might be. Well, it is simple. Everyone needs to realize that they can start from anywhere to reach where they wish their journey through life to lead them. While I may have relocated from Africa many years ago, I still embrace and celebrate African cultures and heritage, along with volunteering my service to various causes that support children in Africa. I believe that the empowerment of at least one child is similar to extending the light of a burning candle to those who might not have been lit up yet, and that is why all that I do pours from my heart.

My intention behind writing this book is to shed some light on the historical perceptions of women and how these have evolved over time to provide an array of opportunities while also showcasing the enduring strength and limitless capabilities of women. The societal norms and misconceptions that once suppressed women's abilities will also form part of the content that you will be reading, where the significance of gender equality and empowerment will be highlighted. The oppression that women have faced for many years might be gradually falling away, but women need the inspiration to embrace the inner strength they possess by standing up and striving for a more balanced and equitable society.

What You Can Expect

There is a long history of oppression and subjugation that continues to filter into the present-day lives of women all across the world. Even though this is most apparent in ancient eras, it begs the question of why this is still a common theme in our modern society. There is a great need to educate society on the appreciation of everyone's contribution to society to sustain this for future generations to come. It is one thing for us to assume that what we do today is only for our benefit, but we need to always be mindful that the coexistence of all who form part of this world requires that we continuously strive to form cohesive societies in the process of us pursuing our passions or finding our purpose in life.

Patriarchal norms have persisted for so many years that women's rights and opportunities they could explore have often been disregarded. This is seen in how there are countries that still enforce child marriages, where young girls are coerced into marrying older men who could qualify to be their uncles or fathers. Some young girls are restricted from going to school, limiting their access to quality education to advance themselves in the world. These are just some examples, but more will be highlighted further in the book.

Chapter 1 will begin by helping us unpack the biblical aspect of women's positioning and how women have been perceived within the biblical context in accordance with societal perceptions. The teachings within the Bible have also influenced how women are viewed, and their relevance in modern gender discussions will be highlighted.

Chapter 2 provides an overview of the journey that has shaped women from years of oppression to the attainment of liberation. Elaborating on some of the societal changes that have transpired will help us understand the path that women have taken over the years to achieve self-empowerment. Systemic barriers that have hindered the progress of women will be discussed, with a focus on how these barriers have exposed women to the harshest treatment.

Chapter 3 will reinforce the title of this book, *The Strength of a Woman*, by analyzing the definitions and expectations that are tied to womanhood and femininity. The power that women possess is often overlooked rather than encouraged, and the evolutionary gender roles that history has shaped over the years will be explored. The distortion of women's self-perception and loss of identity is mainly attributed to traditional gender roles that persist. The need to embrace diverse forms of femininity and redefine gender norms will be covered in this chapter.

Chapter 4 will look at women's enduring strength through their resilience and their ability to triumph over adversity. Not only will this chapter help women understand their worth, but it will emphasize the need for this worth to be realized from within before it can be recognized by others. Obstacles are inevitable in all our lives, but how we choose to overcome these or run away from them is also indicative of our willingness (or unwillingness) to shape the change we wish to see. The support of a community is vital in anyone's life, and women need this also to prevent any psycho-emotional hindrances from setting in.

Chapter 5 will be a continuation of chapter 4 although it will center on the empowerment that women need in the twenty-first century. There are so many roles that women undertake, and each of these bears a contributing factor toward shaping them into who they wish to become. The role of education, advocating for self-love and self-acceptance, and striving for professional opportunities that are sometimes reduced to "being for men" are some of the key points that will be highlighted in this chapter. Selflessness, compassion for others, willingness to forgive, and always striving to maintain peace are some of the inherent qualities that most women possess, and these need to be reinforced with each passing day.

Purpose behind this book

While this book has been written with women in mind, it is necessary for men to equally become more actively involved in the challenges that women encounter daily since we can only shape a conducive society with everyone's equal involvement in this transformational process. So as you read through the book, try to identify any contexts that may be relatable to you and question what has changed since these occurrences, where they are still persisting, and what needs to be done to bring about the necessary change.

*****

*We continue to live amongst **Wonderful Originators** of **Multifaceted Abilities and Notions**, and there's no reason why we shouldn't hold ourselves accountable for ensuring that they realize their full potential without any unnecessary barriers being placed before them.*

Chapter 1

Unveiling Strength through a Biblical Lens

Behind every successful woman is a God who strengthens her. Just like Esther, may you embrace your inner courage and reveal the strength that resides within you.

Nothing in the world can ever prepare you to be a woman when every journey you embark on may have external influences that either contribute positively or negatively to your self-perception. For many women, finding their identity is a process because of the constructs that society tends to hold women to while disregarding the fact that women have their own voice, and their ability to express themselves freely should never be restricted by anything or anyone.

From as far back as the biblical era, men have been depicted as superior beings in contrast to women. This has caused a grave distortion of how women are viewed. In the Bible, women play important roles in stories that show their strengths, weaknesses, and challenges they faced. Take the story of Esther, which is found in Esther 4:16. It depicts a brave woman who risked her life to save her people. This tale teaches us about courage and loyalty, traits that hold value in society. In Genesis 21:1, Sarah's story of facing struggles with infertility until she later bore a child in her old age reflects the power of faith and perseverance that women possess.

Both of these biblical examples mirror the societal expectations of women and men, where women are often portrayed as nurturing and supportive figures. Take the example of Ruth in the book of Ruth, who cared for her mother-in-law, Naomi. This is a beautiful account of loyalty and devotion, whereas women such as Delilah and Jezebel are depicted as manipulative and deceitful, reflecting societal fears of female power and influence. Delilah, who is known for betraying Samson by uncovering his strength in Judges 16, went on to contribute to his downfall. Jezebel, on the other hand, was the wife of King Ahab and was infamous for her deceptive and cunning actions through promoting the worship of false gods and persecuting the prophets of the Lord.

The importance of analyzing the depiction of women in key biblical stories helps us draw parallels with societal norms as this assists with recognizing the significance of biblical narratives in shaping societal perceptions of women and gender roles.

Depiction of Women in Key Biblical Stories and Societal Norms

When considering the portrayal of women in stories like Eve in the Garden of Eden, light is shed on historical gender perceptions and expectations. This narrative has shaped societal views on women's roles, agency, and autonomy while influencing how women are viewed and treated in present-day contexts. The story of Eve highlights power dynamics and prejudices that have lingered through generations, impacting women's empowerment and representation in various spheres. While Eve was the first woman created by and in the image of God, she is regarded as the mother of all living beings and also the originator of sin for having eaten the forbidden fruit from the tree of knowledge of good and evil, along with Adam. This story is captured in Genesis 3:16, and even though she repented for this sin, women are still reminded of this act whenever they are found of any wrongdoing in the present day.

This highlights how even though Eve's story is from many years ago, it is still used as a collective depiction of women's actions of disobedience, unrighteousness, or the ease at which women fall for temptation. This is what makes it particularly important to understand the societal implications of biblical women's roles and the insights that they can offer us into the evolution of gender dynamics. Comparing the roles of biblical women to contemporary views of women can reveal a shift in the expectations and opportunities for women through a lens from different eras.

Christian teachings on the role of women draw from various biblical texts and interpretations, where a lot of dialogue revolves around the significance of women in the Bible and how their roles have been perceived. The Bible often presents both women who hold significant roles, such as Deborah and Esther, and narratives where women are more marginalized. For instance, in the New Testament, some passages discuss the submission of women to their husbands, along with the distinction between the religious roles of men and women. In her 2021 article titled "Ancient Christianity's Effect on Society and Gender Roles," Rebecca Denova explains how men's "primary role was marriage and procreation [while] women were generally allocated one role and contribution to society—their fertility."

The responsibility of the day-to-day running of the household, caring for the children, and child-bearing were seen as the primary roles of women. These types of perceptions have largely misinformed the views held over women and their roles, which also tend to have an impact on their contributions not being taken into account. This is why it becomes imperative to explore how biblical stories influence cultural attitudes toward women as these can help us understand societal beliefs about gender roles by examining how women are portrayed in religious texts versus how they are treated in daily life. This helps with revealing any discrepancies or similarities in viewpoints.

The continuous discussions on how biblical stories influence cultural attitudes toward women and their roles in different contexts can help us understand how religious teachings continue to shape how women are expected to behave or be treated based on these interpretations. This showcases how religious texts also influence societal expectations in modern contexts. There is a need to reflect on how biblical teachings can demonstrate the historical portrayals of women through romantic relationships and family dynamics and their influence on present-day perceptions.

Impact of biblical teachings on gender roles

A continuous examination of the impact of biblical teachings on gender roles and their relevance in modern gender discussions is crucial as this is beneficial to understanding the ongoing relevance of biblical teachings in shaping discourse on gender and empowerment. The Bible often portrays men as providers and protectors of their families while women are depicted as caretakers and nurturing figures. Despite the passage of time, such biblical teachings on gender roles still hold relevance in contemporary society since many people turn to these teachings for moral guidance and ethical principles.

When traditional views on gender roles are being challenged, the Bible tends to be used for reference to either support or challenge a particular viewpoint. These viewpoints are often justifications for upholding certain beliefs on gender equality or when arguing for the preservation of these traditional norms. However, it is important to analyze the evolution of gender roles so we don't conform to stagnant practices but see how they can become more flexible and adaptable to changing generational values.

Biblical teachings should not only be viewed in a contentious light as they sometimes lend themselves to emphasizing virtues such as strength, courage, and kindness. A sense of purpose and empowerment can be cultivated through understanding and relating to contexts that apply to your life. A common mistake many people make is limiting their beliefs based on someone else's experience and disregarding their personal experiences. This prevents any opportunity to learn new ways of thinking and reduces the possibility of overcoming one's adversities without being fearful.

The Bible carries stories that offer empowerment such as Deborah's story of female leadership highlighted in the book of Judges, chapters 4 to 5. She was a prophetess and a judge in Israel who played a significant role in rallying the Israelites to fight against their oppressors and led them to victory. These are stories that you will not hear much about as they portray a woman in a leadership position, which is something that is not readily expected of women. Such stories need to be amplified to show every woman and man that every living being's position is one in which they set their mind and capabilities to achieve a goal that will enrich many successfully.

It is important to note that equality is deeply rooted in the Bible. The endorsement of gender inequality in some passages should not overshadow the emphasis that is placed on the inherent worth and dignity of all individuals, irrespective of their gender. The intersection of faith and gender discussions is complex and multifaceted. Biblical teachings forming the basis for moral and ethical frameworks influence how individuals perceive gender roles. The exploration of this intersection can help people better understand the diverse perspectives that exist.

Stories of strong, assertive women and compassionate, nurturing men in the Bible offer alternative models of gender behavior. In modern society, applying biblical principles to gender discussions continues to spark debates and reflective thought. Some advocate for a return to traditional gender roles based on biblical teachings while others seek to interpret these teachings in light of progressive values.

Looking at how the teachings from the Bible have shaped traditional beliefs about gender roles, it is evident that these ancient texts hold significant influence over societal perceptions. The stories and teachings within the Bible have often been interpreted in a way that reinforces certain expectations about the roles and behavior of individuals. For example, the biblical narrative of Adam and Eve is frequently used to support the idea of men being the breadwinners and women being their supportive counterparts.

When looking into the connections between how biblical texts are understood and contemporary conversations around gender equality, it is crucial also to examine how these views have evolved over time. For scholars such as Richard Sorensen, in his 2024 article titled "Gender and the Bible," an argument is made surrounding the insights that can support efforts toward gender equality. Sorensen (2024) indicates that by critically engaging with biblical texts, individuals can navigate intersections between biblical interpretations and the pursuit of equal rights for all genders in today's world.

Many Christian views on gender and sexuality are deeply rooted in biblical teachings, where the interpretation of these teachings can vary among different denominations and scholars, leading to diverse perspectives on issues like transgender identity. Understanding transgender identity from a biblical perspective is essential for parents who are navigating this topic with their children since it involves exploring the teachings of the Bible and applying them to contemporary issues related to gender and identity.

Parents can approach discussions about gender using biblical principles of love, compassion, and understanding. Encouraging open dialogue and providing a safe space for children to express their thoughts and questions are welcomed. Challenges may arise when having to explain transgender identity to children within the context of Christian beliefs. However, offering support, seeking guidance from pastoral leaders, and fostering empathy can help navigate these complex discussions.

Questions surrounding self-expression, gender fluidity, and inclusivity are becoming increasingly relevant in today's society, prompting individuals to reflect on how biblical stories contribute to or challenge prevailing norms. When discussing the challenges and opportunities presented by biblical perspectives on gender roles in today's society, it is essential to address the complexities that arise from reconciling ancient texts with contemporary values. While some view biblical teachings as restrictive or outdated in their portrayal of gender dynamics, others find inspiration in stories of resilience, equality, and social justice within these texts. By engaging in open dialogues that acknowledge both the limitations and possibilities presented by biblical perspectives, individuals can navigate the complexities of gender debates with a more informed and inclusive approach.

Today's definition of women

Women today are seen in a different light compared to women in the past. Today, women are considered to have more freedom in various aspects of life and are often encouraged to pursue their education and career goals, and this gives them more independence and opportunities to make choices for themselves. Whereas in the past, women were mainly expected to fulfill domestic roles without much say in societal matters. In modern society, women have more educational opportunities available to them, allowing them to attend schools and universities, pursue degrees in various fields, and have successful careers in industries that were previously dominated by men.

We are in an age where women are now CEOs, doctors, engineers, lawyers, and presidents and hold positions of power and influence. This is in direct contrast to their position in the past, where they were discouraged from seeking education or entering workforces. There is more independence and autonomy in decision-making, which is notable in how women can choose their own partners, make informed financial decisions, have the right to vote, own property, and determine the course of their lives. This drastic shift reflects a greater recognition of women's rights and equality in modern times. In the past, women could only dream of seeking recognition or autonomy beyond the roles they were expected to be limited to, where their personal priorities were barely ever acknowledged.

The expectation that women should be submissive and obedient to male figures only served to reinforce patriarchal values, which relegated women to subordinate positions. The evolution of the definition of women today in comparison to the past reflects how women have gained greater recognition and rights, allowing them to pursue paths that were once inaccessible to them. By recognizing the complexities and contradictions inherent in comparing biblical women's roles with societal norms, we can appreciate the progress made in empowering women and shaping more inclusive and equitable communities.

Drawing parallels between biblical women and women in different cultures

In many cultures, women are often expected to fulfill specific roles based on societal norms and traditions. Similarly, in biblical stories, women are often depicted in roles that align with the values and expectations of their time. For instance, women in ancient societies were responsible for tasks that were seen as being essential for maintaining order and stability within the community. Despite advancements in promoting gender equality, women continue to face challenges in breaking away from traditional roles and stereotypes. The cultural expectations and pressures placed on them often limit their freedom to explore alternative roles and opportunities. However, the progress made in advocating for women's rights and empowerment has paved the way for gender inclusivity and diversity in women's roles.

The roles and experiences of women are also influenced by factors such as race, ethnicity, religion, and social class. When viewing biblical narratives, we can observe instances where gender stereotypes are challenged and reinforced. For example, the story of Ruth and Naomi depicts the bond between women, which challenges the notion that women are solely defined by their relationships with men. On the other hand, stories like the submission of Sarah to Abraham may reinforce traditional gender roles by emphasizing obedience and submissiveness.

The gender dynamics portrayed in biblical stories offer a glimpse into the complexities of relationships between men and women. For example, the story of Deborah, a prophetess and judge, challenges traditional gender norms by showcasing a woman in a position of authority and leadership (which is still shunned in this day and age). This shows that women in ancient societies were not only mothers and wives, but they were leaders and heroines. The consideration of the relevance of such narratives to contemporary discussions is necessary, especially when you look at the stories of Esther, Ruth, or Mary Magdalene, since these offer insights into the struggles and triumphs of women in a patriarchal society.

Scholars and researchers delve into the intersection of gender and the Bible by examining ancient texts and historical contexts to gain insights into the portrayal of gender roles. Studying these connections contributes to a deeper understanding of biblical teachings on gender. Academic studies shed light on the historical and cultural factors that shaped biblical perspectives on gender. The exploration of gender in the Bible carries implications for contemporary discussions on women's roles, gender equality, and LGBTQ+ issues. By revisiting biblical texts through a scholarly lens, individuals can gain a more nuanced understanding of these complex topics to simplify them for others further.

Contrasting perspectives—definitions of women in modern gender discussions

While historical definitions of women can be seen as undermining, these are crucial to help us realize the progress that has been made in women's rights and the acknowledgment of gender equality. As society evolves, so do the definitions of women and their roles. The challenges in redefining women's identities lie in dismantling stereotypes and biases that have been ingrained in cultures for centuries. The power of words is also important when defining women since this shapes the gender discourse as words have the power to reinforce the stereotypes or trump them. By critically examining the language we use to define women, we can foster more inclusive and empowering dialogues that reflect the diversity of women's experiences.

By recognizing and celebrating the various ways in which women define themselves, we move toward a more inclusive and equitable society that challenges binary conceptions of gender. Women continue to assert their right to define themselves, where this autonomy of self-definition promotes inclusivity while capturing the uniqueness of each woman's identity. We need to understand that gender equality is a collective responsibility that requires everyone to engage in ongoing conversations about the definition of women in society.

When we talk about gender and power in the olden days, looking at biblical tales can help us see how men's and women's portrayals differed significantly. When looking at how Eve faced consequences for her and Adam's actions in the Garden of Eden, you see how women were easily stigmatized. When using biblical references to discuss gender equality and social justice, we need to consider the context in which these stories were written. For instance, debates on LGBTQ+ rights may involve references to Sodom and Gomorrah, but interpreting these stories requires understanding the historical and cultural context in which they were written.

The destruction of Sodom and Gomorrah, as highlighted in Genesis chapters 18 to 19, can be viewed in relation to LGBTQ+ topics as the condemnation of homosexuality, hospitality, abuse, and justice ties into the moral lessons and implications of the story. By reimagining these stories through a feminist lens, we can find new meanings and messages that resonate with contemporary views on gender equality. While this chapter focused on unveiling women's strength through a biblical lens, it also drew contrasts between past and present definitions of women. The next chapter will expand on this by exploring the journey from oppression to liberation and how the path to empowerment has been paved for women from diverse walks of life.

*****

*The true potential of wisdom can be derived from a **Wise Oracle Mastering Authority Now**, as she will always guide you on a path of understanding the past, to make sense of the present and gain clarity for the future.*

Chapter 2

From Oppression to Liberation: A Path to Empowerment

*From the shackles of oppression to the wings of
liberation, women have paved a path of empowerment
that resonates with courage, resilience, and
unwavering strength. May every stride they take be
a testament to the radiant freedom that comes from
breaking barriers and embracing their true power.*

Navigating the journey toward self-empowerment and societal change can be one of the most challenging endeavors in anyone's life, but it is inevitable to reach a point in your life that necessitates this of you. Self-empowerment is mainly about feeling confident and capable in your abilities, which requires you to recognize your worth and believe in yourself. It also entails taking control of your life decisions and actions by setting personal goals that you should strive to achieve. Taking the necessary steps to achieve these goals is how you practice self-empowerment.

Another way to cultivate self-empowerment is through self-reflection, which requires you to look inward and examine your thoughts and feelings to understand yourself better. Taking care of your physical, emotional, and mental well-being, along with engaging in activities that promote relaxation and reduce stress, are some of the vital self-care practices that encourage you to maintain a healthy mindset.

These are some of the key aspects that women in the past never had a chance to fully embrace, given how there wasn't much advocacy or promotion of the need for personal care. Women have historically been viewed as holding back progress in society, where their potential contributions would often be overlooked. This is why a need to acknowledge women's voices and dismantle any barriers that prevented them from actively contributing to society arose.

The systemic barriers that previously existed need to be recognized since they are the main contributor to women's hindered progress. Some of the barriers that were highlighted in a 2022 article by Media Relations specify that these were in the form of unequal pay, limited access to education and healthcare, a lack of representation in leadership roles, along gender stereotypes that still prevail in present-day society. The most significant barrier is the wage gap between women and their male counterparts, which reflects a lack of economic empowerment and perpetuates cycles of poverty and dependence.

The issue of access to education and health care is another critical aspect that also contributes to a lack of progress that can be seen in the advancement of women as the denial of education to young girls in some parts of the world means that they are denied educational opportunities, which leads to limited skills development. The inadequate access to quality health-care services can have detrimental effects on women's well-being and their overall quality of life since you still find that some women are unaware of the changes they experience during puberty or feel scared to discuss anything relating to sexual encounters, abstinence, or even conception. These are topics that are still quite taboo in this day and age as women tend to be stigmatized over the natural cycles they undergo because of insufficient avenues being available for them to openly speak about the transformations that occur to, within, and through their bodies.

The underrepresentation of women in leadership positions is also a reinforcement of the limitations on diverse perspectives and experiences as well as the notion that women are less capable or deserving of leadership roles. A move toward the empowerment of women would require an increase in the representation of women in leadership roles through proactive measures such as promoting mentorship programs, implementing diversity quotas, and openly challenging traditional norms that discourage women from seeking leadership positions.

What can be noted from rigid gender norms is their perpetuation of discrimination and restrictions on freedom of choice, and they impede women's ability to explore their full potential. Through the establishment of more supportive environments, women will start realizing that a shift is being made from ancient views of women, and the cultivation of respect, empowerment, and equality will become evident to enable women to thrive and contribute meaningfully to society's advancement.

From Oppression to Present Day

Societies such as ancient Greece and Rome often viewed women primarily as caretakers of the home and family and restricted women's participation in public life. However, even within these constraints, there emerged exceptional figures who defied societal norms, showcasing early signs of resistance and pioneering change. As we move through the Middle Ages, which spanned approximately from the fifth to the fifteenth century, women's roles began to diversify although many still faced considerable limitations. Noblewomen could exercise their influence through marriage alliances and estate management, yet their societal contributions remained overshadowed by patriarchal values. Similarly, peasant women labored alongside men, contributing to the agricultural economy but without equal recognition or rights. This era witnessed the gradual surfacing of women's voices, where this lay the foundation for future movements.

The Renaissance period, between the fourteenth and seventeenth centuries, brought a renewed interest in arts and sciences, which partly translated into more educational opportunities for women in affluent circles. Women like Artemisia Gentileschi and Sofonisba Anguissola made their mark in the art world, proving that when women are given the chance, they can excel in intellectual and creative pursuits. The Enlightenment that occurred in the seventeenth and eighteenth centuries further opened doors as ideas about human rights and individual liberty gained traction. Thinkers like Mary Wollstonecraft persistently argued for women's education and equality, influencing subsequent generations. It was during this time that the seeds of the modern feminist movement were sown to advocate for the intrinsic value and potential of every woman. Moving into the nineteenth and early twentieth centuries, the women's battle for suffrage epitomized a crucial chapter in the quest for equality as women worldwide mobilized and demonstrated courage and unwavering determination. Leaders like Susan B. Anthony and Emmeline Pankhurst became symbols of empowerment through their efforts, resulting in substantial legislative transformations, including the right to vote.

The mid-twentieth century saw the rise of the second wave of feminism, which sought not only legal equality but also social and economic justice. Women challenged traditional roles, demanding reproductive rights and an end to gender discrimination. Figures like Simone de Beauvoir and Betty Friedan inspired many other women to scrutinize and dismantle oppressive structures. The impact of these movements spread globally. Today, we observe a more complex and multifaceted landscape, and while significant strides have been made, challenges remain. Reflecting on this journey from oppression to empowerment, it becomes clear that each era contributed uniquely to the evolving narrative of women's roles. The unwavering spirit of women who fought for their rights continually propels us forward to ensure that even when we are faced with obstacles, we can persist and maintain an unshakeable belief in our worth and capabilities.

Women's Advancement in the Face of Societal Norms and Structures

The creation of women has been seen for too long as a hindrance to society's advancement, but they have been subjected to the harshest treatment. Societal norms are the unwritten rules that guide how we behave in society, like how women are expected to focus more on family than a career. Many women face challenges because of these norms as they are expected to prioritize household duties over pursuing professional goals.

By understanding how societal norms and structures create obstacles to women's advancement, individuals can begin to challenge and break through these barriers. For example, recognizing that women are often not encouraged to take leadership roles in certain industries can inspire women to actively seek out such opportunities and advocate for their place at the table. This can greatly empower women to push back against the status quo as we've seen with Mexico's newly elected first female president, Claudia Sheinbaum. While she may be faced with numerous challenges because she's a woman, she has the opportunity to advance reforms that will not only prioritize gender roles but promote a new perspective for women to be respected in leadership roles.

The role of mentorship is very vital in helping women navigate societal structures as this will aid them in overcoming similar challenges through the valuable insights and advice they stand to gain from it. Connecting with like-minded individuals who can offer support and opportunities for growth will help spearhead gender equity while also helping women become confident through having access to the necessary resources to forge their path toward success.

There's a need to motivate women to pursue further education in male-dominated fields since this will equip them with the skills they need to excel in their careers despite the prevailing norms and expectations. Women, like everyone else, deserve a workspace that creates an environment that allows them to thrive, and organizations need to foster a culture that values differences, encourages respect, and offers support where it may be needed.

Where it may be necessary, policy changes and legislative measures need to be enforceable as these may dismantle societal obstacles for women and ensure that they are being fairly treated. The cultivation of a sense of self-belief is also vital since women overcome barriers through their perseverance to stand for what is right while being able to point out what is not right. By building resilience in the face of adversity, women are able to bounce back from failures, learn valuable lessons from their shortcomings, and continue pursuing their goals regardless of any external barriers that may be present.

You will note how women's collective action and solidarity have proven to be useful in advancing the plight for the equal and full recognition of women within society. Some noteworthy historical examples are the following:

1. The American Civil Rights Movement that took place between the 1950s and 1960s involved women like Rosa Parks and Fannie Lou Hamer, who were instrumental in the fight for civil rights, alongside male leaders like Martin Luther King, Jr. This movement was sparked by the Montgomery bus boycott, following Rosa Parks's refusal "to give up her seat on a public bus to a White man" (Carson 2024).

2. The Indian Independence Movement, which primarily took place between 1857 and 1947, saw women like Sarojini Naidu, Rani Lakshmibai, and Kamala Nehru actively participating in India's struggle for independence, alongside Mahatma Gandhi. These women-led "resistance against British forces, inspired masses with speeches, [advocated] for nonviolent resistance, organized and led

protests, [and] advocated for women's rights and social reform" (Rishi 2024).

3. The Women's Suffrage Movement, which began in the mid-nineteenth century and continued into the early twentieth century in countries like the United States, the United Kingdom, and many others, saw women fighting for the right to vote, which led to significant political reform.

4. The Anti-Apartheid Movement, which took place in South Africa during the mid-twentieth century and gained momentum in the 1950s through to the drawing to an end of the apartheid regime in the 1990s, had Winnie Madikizela-Mandela and Albertina Sisulu playing a vital role in the struggle to abolish apartheid, alongside leaders like Nelson Mandela and Walter Sisulu (who were also their husbands).

5. The women's rights movements that have been happening for centuries for political and social transformations have been gaining traction in various parts of the world at different times. These ongoing movements are mainly for gender equality and women's rights globally to challenge societal norms and advocate for women's empowerment and liberation.

All these are examples that depict how women have been actively involved in the transformational processes of gaining liberty and ensuring that society recognizes this as well. This reinforces the need for policy, political, economic, and societal reform as all of these directly contribute to women's placement within societies.

There is an increased need for workplaces and institutions, in general, to create fair opportunities for everyone since the promotion of inclusivity is crucial for the sustainability of any environment. Companies need to work toward implementing policies that address gender disparities in workspaces, where these can also be adopted within educational institutions. By adopting such policies, companies will ensure that women are paid fairly, provide flexible work arrangements, and provide parental leave to support working mothers who need to balance their responsibilities at work and at home.

Training and education are compulsory for employees as workshops and seminars help raise awareness about unconscious bias and gender stereotypes. This will greatly assist employees in understanding the importance of gender equity in creating a more harmonious workplace culture. In some instances, even collaborating with advocacy groups could prove to be beneficial since those that focus on gender equity can amplify efforts to address systemic issues affecting women's opportunities. Companies stand to leverage the expertise of these advocacy groups as their expertise and resources can drive meaningful change.

The promotion of leadership training initiatives, mentorship programs, and networking opportunities that are designed to empower and advance women in leadership roles will empower them to form part of more inclusive environments. Inclusivity is sustained through fostering open communication to encourage employees to voice their opinions and share their experiences with each other. This is the best way for companies to not only attract people from diverse backgrounds but also to retain top talent.

It is important to regularly monitor and evaluate the impact of gender equity initiatives to ensure that progress is being made as this helps with identifying areas for improvement. By tracking key performance indicators related to gender representation, pay equity, and the satisfaction of employees, companies can measure the effectiveness of their efforts and make decisions that are driven by the data presented to them to promote gender equity not only in the present but in the long term as well. The promotion of gender equity is an ongoing process that requires continuous effort and commitment, so the continuation of the conversation can help raise awareness, advocate for change, and inspire others to take action to create a more equitable and inclusive society for all.

Gender, race, and class are crucial aspects of one's identity that influence how one experiences the world. When people talk about intersectionality, they are referring to how these different aspects intersect and overlap, where unique experiences for individuals are created. Fair opportunities can only be created within equitable environments by making them more inclusive, respectful, and educational in the intersectionality of gender, class, and race to raise more awareness of the complexities that women face.

Everyone's identity is largely influenced by their experience of the world, where each person's differences intersect or overlap in a unique way. When taking a closer look at the crucial aspects that define a person's identity, discrimination and marginalization are often encountered by women from different racial and socioeconomic backgrounds. We can consider the example of how women of color tend to be treated differently to women from other racial groups, and this fosters unhealthy divisions among women when they basically face similar hardships in their daily lives.

Jessie Kwak (2021) alludes to the promotion of equity in the classroom with intersectional pedagogy, where she highlights that the range of identities found in the classrooms need to be intersected to gain different experiences from each individual. Jessie further adds that "traumatic experiences or a history of systemic educational inequity are less readily apparent," and this requires the acknowledgment of the intersecting identities of students, the inclusion of their cultural experiences, especially in aspects of learning, and that classrooms need to be designed "with a range of identities in mind" (Kwak 2021).

Women's empowerment in societal equality

Imagine the intricate threads that weave together to form a tapestry, where each thread represents an identity, such as gender, race, or class. When we look at women's experiences, these threads don't exist in isolation but are tightly interwoven, creating a complex and unique pattern for each individual. This interconnectedness is what we refer to as *intersectionality*, a term introduced by Kimberlé Crenshaw to describe how different aspects of a person's identity combine to shape their social experiences and outcomes.

The problem arises when societal structures fail to recognize these overlapping identities, leading to a one-size-fits-all approach that often overlooks the needs of many women. For example, while some feminist movements have historically focused on the struggles of White, middle-class women, they have frequently ignored the barriers faced by women of color or those from lower economic backgrounds. Statistics show that while women generally earn less than men, the wage gap is even more significant for Black and Hispanic women, who earn only about sixty-four cents and fifty-six cents respectively for every dollar earned by a White man. Additionally, health-care disparities, housing challenges, and educational inequities further compound the issues faced by marginalized groups, making it evident that a more nuanced understanding is necessary.

We need to start recognizing that it is not just about being a woman; it is about being a Black woman, a Latina woman, an Asian woman, a working-class woman, or a woman with disabilities. Each layer of identity brings its own set of challenges and experiences, which overlap and influence one another. Historically, many feminist movements largely focused on the issues of White, middle-class women. This approach overlooked the unique struggles faced by women of color, those from lower-income backgrounds, and other marginalized groups. For instance, while it is commonly stated that women earn seventy-eight cents for every dollar earned by men, this doesn't paint the full picture. Black women earn about sixty-four cents, and Hispanic women only earn fifty-six cents to a White man's dollar (Hawk et al. 2016). These discrepancies highlight why it is crucial to adopt an intersectional perspective.

When you consider the plight of Sojourner Truth, a former slave who became an outspoken advocate for abolition and women's rights, you get to learn of her famous speech, "Ain't I a Woman?" which was delivered in 1851, to question the exclusion of Black women from the women's suffrage movement. She expressed how her experiences as a Black woman were distinctly different from those of White women, emphasizing that both her race and gender needed to be acknowledged. Fast-forward to contemporary times, where this struggle still continues. When viewing the disparity in earnings, you realize that it is not just a result of gender discrimination, but it is compounded by racial biases and economic inequalities.

Women of color often find themselves in lower-paying jobs with less security and fewer benefits compared to their White counterparts, reflecting a combination of gendered racism and economic injustice.

Intersectionality plays a vital role in understanding health-care disparities. Studies have shown that Black women are three to four times more likely to die from pregnancy-related causes than White women. This alarming statistic is not solely about access to health care, but it reflects systemic racism within institutions, socioeconomic status, and gender bias. The interwoven nature of these factors creates a more dangerous environment for Black mothers. Housing is another area where intersectionality is apparent as women often face eviction at higher rates than men. This trend can be traced back to discriminatory housing policies and practices that target low-income communities and people of color.

During the subprime mortgage crisis, borrowers of color were disproportionately given high-cost loans compared to White borrowers with similar credit scores. This led to higher foreclosure rates among Black and Latin families, resulting in economic instability and housing insecurity for women in these communities. The underfunding that is evident in predominantly Black and Latin neighborhoods seems to have negative implications on the quality of education as seen in the availability of resources and the overall school environment. Girls of color are often subjected to harsher disciplinary measures, lowering their academic performance and self-esteem. These consequences hinder their chances of pursuing higher education and better job opportunities.

Understanding intersectionality is not just about recognizing these problems but also about advocating for comprehensive solutions. Policies aimed at gender equality must consider race and class to be effective. Gender-neutral policies often fail to address the specific needs of women of color or those from disadvantaged backgrounds. For instance, workplace policies must go beyond addressing gender bias to include anti-racist training and support for economic mobility. This will ensure that inclusive environments are created to listen to the voices of all women, especially those from marginalized groups, and to examine our privileges and biases by actively seeking out diverse perspectives. This will provide us with a lens through which we can better understand the multifaceted experiences of women and work toward establishing a society where every woman's voice is not just heard but valued too.

Navigating challenges and embracing self-empowerment

The various challenges women face due to societal structures and norms are deeply rooted in traditional gender roles and expectations. These norms not only shape how society views women but also how women see themselves, impacting their opportunities and self-esteem. Globally, restrictive gender norms limit women's potential and opportunities for growth. For instance, many young girls are discouraged from pursuing careers in STEM fields because these areas are traditionally seen as male-dominated. They might hear comments that suggest they are better suited for caregiving or artistic roles, shaping their career aspirations and limiting their choices.

In everyday life, women often juggle numerous roles—from being primary caregivers at home to professional responsibilities. Society expects them to balance these roles effortlessly, often without adequate support or recognition. This expectation can lead to significant stress, burnout, and even health issues. Moreover, the lack of affordable childcare forces many women to either leave their jobs or accept lower-paying positions that offer flexibility, further widening the economic gap between men and women. Despite these obstacles, women continue to find ways to empower themselves and overcome societal barriers. Self-empowerment begins with recognizing one's own worth and capabilities. It is crucial for women to believe in their potential and seek opportunities for personal and professional growth.

Here are some of the ways that women can consider to achieve any goals they set for themselves:

- Seek out mentors and role models who inspire you and provide guidance on navigating challenges.
- Surround yourself with a supportive network of friends and family who encourage your aspirations.

- Invest in your education and skill development to open up more career opportunities.
- Advocate for yourself in the workplace by negotiating salaries, promotions, and fair treatment.
- Practice self-care to maintain your mental and physical well-being. Prioritize activities that rejuvenate and energize you.

These steps can help women cultivate resilience and confidence, enabling them to face societal expectations head-on and carve out paths toward their goals. Embracing self-empowerment is not just about individual success; it is about inspiring others and fostering a culture where women can support each other. Corporations and governments also have a pivotal role in breaking down gender norms and creating equitable opportunities. Implementing policies like paid maternity and paternity leave, flexible working hours, and affordable childcare can significantly impact women's ability to thrive both personally and professionally.

Companies must foster inclusive cultures where gender diversity is celebrated and women are encouraged to take on leadership roles. Diverse teams bring varied perspectives, enhancing creativity and problem-solving. On an organizational level, it is crucial to provide training on gender sensitivity and unconscious biases to ensure a respectful work environment for everyone. Schools and universities are starting points for challenging gender norms since they should promote gender-neutral curricula and encourage students to pursue interests regardless of their gender. Teachers play a crucial role here by refraining from reinforcing stereotypes and actively supporting all students in their pursuits. Introducing students to diverse role models through books, guest speakers, and media can help dismantle stereotypical images of what men and women can achieve. Schools should also provide safe spaces for discussions around gender, race, and class, fostering an environment of understanding and respect.

The media has immense power in shaping societal perceptions as they need to portray women in diverse roles by moving away from traditional stereotypes. Strong, independent female characters in TV shows, movies, and advertisements can inspire young girls to dream bigger and break free from societal constraints. Media should also highlight stories of women who have overcome significant challenges, showcasing their journeys and achievements. By doing so, they provide relatable examples of resilience and success, motivating others to follow suit.

Communities also play a pivotal role in supporting women's empowerment. Local organizations, women's groups, and advocacy networks offer resources, workshops, and events focused on personal and professional development. These groups create a sense of belonging and collective strength, helping women realize they are not alone in their struggles. By joining or forming support groups, women are provided with a platform for sharing experiences, exchanging advice, and building confidence. Community initiatives can also target policy changes at the local level, advocating for measures that promote gender equality and support women's rights. While societal structures and norms present significant challenges for women, strategies for self-empowerment and external support can pave the way for overcoming these obstacles. By working together and challenging traditional norms, we can create an inclusive and empowering environment for all women.

Strategies for advocacy and change

Understanding the intersectionality of gender, race, and class is crucial for effective advocacy and policy change. Intersecting identities influence experiences in profound ways, and a one-size-fits-all approach to gender equality and social justice simply will not work. One effective approach to the advocacy of gender equality is grassroots organizing. This form of activism starts at the local level, empowering communities to take collective action. Grassroots movements give a voice to those who might otherwise be marginalized by allowing them to influence public policy directly. For instance, local campaigns to improve housing conditions or educational opportunities can lead to broader changes that benefit everyone.

Community organizing is another powerful tool since it brings people together for shared goals, and this approach helps build strong networks of support.

Community organizers work to identify common issues, develop strategies, and mobilize resources, and this often results in significant and lasting improvements in social policies and practices. Public policy advocacy is essential for driving systemic change because policies shape our daily lives from access to health care and education to job opportunities and environmental protections. Advocates for social justice must work to ensure that these policies are fair and equitable by engaging with lawmakers, participating in public hearings, and using data to support arguments for effective policy advocacy.

Activism plays a vital role in highlighting and challenging systemic inequalities as it brings attention to issues that may be overlooked or ignored and pushes for necessary changes. Feminist movements have been instrumental in advancing women's rights and gender equality, and these movements use various strategies, including protests, awareness campaigns, and legal challenges, to fight against discrimination and promote equal opportunities (Oxfam Policy and Practice, n.d.). Similarly, racial justice movements like Black Lives Matter have brought global attention to issues of police brutality, racial profiling, and systemic racism. By mobilizing communities and leveraging the power of social media, these movements have forced policymakers to address long-standing injustices and implement reforms (Yeshiva University 2024).

Effective policy change is a cornerstone of promoting social justice. Policies that consider the needs of diverse populations and address systemic barriers can transform societies. One notable example is the Affordable Care Act (ACA) that was enacted in 2010, which has significantly improved access to health care for millions of Americans, particularly those from marginalized communities. By addressing disparities in health-care access, the ACA has made strides toward a more equitable health system (Yeshiva University 2024). Another important policy is the Every Student Succeeds Act (ESSA), which Barack Obama signed into law in 2015. It aims to close achievement gaps in education by providing resources to underserved schools. Policies like ESSA help ensure that all students, regardless of their background, have access to quality education.

Women's empowerment is a critical aspect of achieving societal equality. Empowered women are more likely to participate fully in economic, social, and political life, leading to a more just and inclusive society. And these are some of the ways that can spur women to realize this goal:

- Support education and training programs that enhance women's skills and knowledge.
- Advocate for equal pay and employment opportunities.
- Encourage women's participation in leadership roles and decision-making processes.
- Promote policies that protect women from violence and discrimination.
- Foster environments that support work-life balance and childcare.

These steps not only empower individual women but also contribute to broader societal progress. It's essential to keep pushing forward by working together to bring about change through evidence and driven by a collective will for transformation. By working together, we can build a world where everyone's rights are respected and upheld, regardless of their gender, race, or class. Creating spaces that are inclusive and supportive of diverse identities is a cornerstone for fostering empowerment and equality. It is not just about opening doors but ensuring that people feel genuinely welcomed and valued when they walk through them. The importance of community support cannot be overstated in this endeavor.

When we talk about inclusivity, it is essential to recognize that everyone brings unique perspectives shaped by their gender, race, and class experiences. For some, the journey to find accepting spaces can be fraught with challenges, and this is why we need to create environments where all individuals, regardless of how they identify or the intersections of their identities, feel seen and respected. One way to foster such spaces is through community gatherings and support groups specifically designed to be inclusive. These gatherings allow people to share their experiences and challenges while finding solidarity and understanding among peers. Such spaces also provide opportunities for learning and growth, helping members better understand the nuanced experiences of others.

In creating these inclusive spaces, it is vital to ensure that all voices are heard and valued equally.

For instance, in meditation groups and daylongs for trans and genderqueer people, creating an environment where everyone feels they belong—regardless of whether they *pass* as cisgender—is crucial. This means holding space for young trans people and trans women who may face targeted discrimination while also honoring everyone's unique identity (Bioneers 2020). Online communities have shown great potential as inclusive spaces, where platforms like YouTube, Instagram, X (formerly Twitter), and TikTok offer resources and connections for those exploring their identities. However, in-person meetings hold a special significance. These meetups offer direct human connection, erasing fears and misconceptions about belonging. It's important to encourage engagement in these real-world communities to strengthen one's sense of self and acceptance.

To build truly inclusive environments, we can take some of the following steps:

- Be intentional about inclusivity in all spaces, whether they are physical or virtual. Make it clear that all identities are welcome and valued.
- Listen actively to the needs and concerns of marginalized community members. Use their feedback to shape policies and practices.
- Encourage visible representation of diverse identities within leadership and participant roles. Representation matters, and seeing

oneself reflected in a community fosters a stronger connection.

- Provide resources and education around inclusivity and intersectionality. This helps all members understand the complexities of different identities and experiences.

Building a supportive community extends beyond just welcoming diverse identities; it's about empowering individuals within those communities. Empowerment comes from feeling accepted and understood, which can significantly impact one's self-confidence and ability to thrive. For those navigating the awkwardness of coming out to family and friends, remember that acceptance often precedes understanding. Family members might need time to adjust and mourn the change they perceive. Encouraging them to respect and accept you as you are can be a significant first step toward improving your relationship.

Creating inclusive spaces also involves recognizing and addressing the discomfort and challenges that come with cultural differences and systemic inequalities. For instance, women from the Middle East navigating predominantly male fields or adapting to new cultures might initially struggle with feelings of exclusion. Fostering their sense of belonging begins with acknowledging these challenges and supporting their endeavors to integrate and succeed (Wilson Center, n.d.). It is crucial to understand that building these inclusive and supportive communities requires collective effort, and collaborations between government, corporations, and grassroots organizations can drive substantial progress. However, checks and balances must be in place to ensure public interests remain at the forefront.

By prioritizing human welfare over mere economic growth, we create environments where all individuals can flourish. Personal responsibility in contributing to and maintaining these inclusive spaces is essential. Simultaneously, there should be a safety net for those encountering hard times, ensuring no one is left behind. Through these efforts, we can cultivate communities where diversity is celebrated, inclusion is the norm, and every member feels empowered and valued. In doing so, we not only enhance individual well-being but also strengthen the fabric of our society as a whole.

Reflections on the path forward

Throughout this chapter, we've explored the intricate intersectionality of gender, race, and class to understand how these layers shape women's experiences. By examining historical and contemporary examples, we've highlighted the unique challenges women face when multiple aspects of their identity come into play. Initially, we discussed how feminist movements often overlooked the struggles of women of color and those from lower economic backgrounds. This oversight has led to a lack of comprehensive understanding and support for all women. As mentioned earlier in the chapter, using an intersectional lens helps us see that not all women face the same issues in the same way.

Our current position is clear: Recognizing the interconnectedness of gender, race, and class is crucial if we want to create effective and inclusive policies and environments. It's not just about acknowledging these intersections but actively working to address them. For example, in areas like health care, education, and employment, we need to consider how systemic biases intersect to impact different groups of women. We should all be concerned about the continuous perpetuation of inequalities if these intersections are ignored. When policies and reforms fail to account for the diverse experiences of all women, they inadvertently uphold existing disparities, and this can lead to broader social consequences, such as perpetuating economic instability and limiting access to essential services for marginalized communities.

On a wider scale, ignoring intersectionality can stifle societal progress. If we don't address the unique challenges faced by various groups of women, our efforts toward equality will remain incomplete and ineffective. We must strive for inclusivity in all aspects of life, ensuring that every woman's voice is heard and valued to ensure that as we move forward, we remain open to learning and growing. Reflect on your own identities and privileges and consider how they influence your perspectives. By doing so, we can foster more inclusive and supportive communities where everyone feels seen and respected. Only then can we hope to achieve true gender equality and social justice.

*****

*We can only become the **Warriors Of** Magnitude, **Ambition**, and **Nobility** by first recognizing this in ourselves to turn it into the reality that we wish to see unfold in our lives.*

CHAPTER 3

Redefining Femininity: The Strength of Women

In a world where boundaries are blurred and norms are challenged, women are rewriting the narrative of femininity and reshaping the expectations of womanhood. They stand tall, unapologetically embracing their diverse identities, challenging stereotypes, and redefining what it means to be truly empowered as a woman.

Throughout history, women have been misrepresented when it comes to their strength. Unlike the idea of force, which is about being aggressive and upfront, women's power is more intricate and quiet. It is the kind of strength that can help communities grow, bring about positive changes, and make societies better places to live. Women have a power that goes beyond what is obvious. It is not just about physical strength but also emotional intelligence, empathy, and resilience. Women have the ability to inspire others, foster relationships, and create nurturing environments where people can thrive. Over time, the concept of femininity has evolved, allowing women to embrace their diverse strengths and abilities. This evolution has led to a redefinition of what it means to be a woman in society as women are no longer confined to traditional roles but are actively participating in leadership, innovation, and social change.

The changes in how femininity is perceived have profoundly impacted society. Women are now driving progress in various fields, breaking barriers, and challenging stereotypes. By recognizing the unique contributions of women, societies are becoming more inclusive, diverse, and equitable. Women's power is not just about individual strength but also about collective empowerment. Women are coming together to support one another, advocate for their rights, and create spaces where everyone's voices are heard. This sense of community and solidarity is creating a ripple effect of positive change.

Women have the ability to inspire change by standing up for justice, fighting for equality, and challenging injustices. By speaking out against discrimination and advocating for fairness, women are shaping a more just and equitable world for future generations. As femininity continues to evolve, the definition of womanhood is also changing. Women are no longer defined by narrow stereotypes but are celebrated for their unique strengths and contributions. This shift in perception allows women to lead with authenticity and confidence, influencing others to do the same.

Traditionally, women were confined to strict roles within the home and expected to be gentle, nurturing, and submissive. These expectations limited their opportunities, reinforcing a narrow definition of femininity focused on domestic responsibilities. Historically, the ideal woman was often depicted as someone who could easily be subjected to domestic duties. Such stereotypes not only shaped how society viewed women but also how women viewed themselves. Girls were taught to play with dolls and embrace nurturing roles from a young age, internalizing these societal messages deeply.

This chapter will explore the evolution of gender roles and their impact on defining femininity by looking at historical shifts such as women's participation in the workforce during the industrial revolution and the influence of media representations. We'll also examine how feminist movements have redefined women's roles and how modern-day discussions continue to challenge traditional norms. By reflecting on these changes, we can better understand the complexities of gender and support diverse expressions of femininity.

The Power of Women

Throughout history, gender roles have significantly influenced societal perceptions of femininity. Traditionally, these roles were rigid, dictating specific behaviors, duties, and attributes as inherently male or female. Women, in particular, were often confined to domestic spheres, expected to embody virtues like nurturing, gentleness, and subservience to fulfill societal expectations. One of the most profound ways historical gender roles shaped views on femininity was through the lens of household responsibilities. Women were primarily seen as homemakers and caregivers. This role not only limited their opportunities but also reinforced a narrow definition of femininity that revolved around family and home. The image of the ideal woman was someone who balanced household chores effortlessly, cared for children, and supported her husband unconditionally.

The influence of traditional gender norms seeped into women's self-perception. From an early age, girls were socialized to adopt behaviors considered feminine. Activities and interests were often divided along gender lines, leading girls to internalize much of their societal experiences and limitations. For instance, they were encouraged to play with dolls rather than trucks, reinforcing a nurturing role from a young age. This early socialization had long-term impacts, setting the stage for how women viewed themselves and their capabilities. During the industrial revolution that started in the late eighteenth century in the United Kingdom to mark a significant period of industrial and technological development, a shift in economic structures began to challenge traditional gender roles. With men working in factories, some women entered the workforce, albeit in limited capacities. Despite this change, the perception of women's primary identity being tied to domesticity persisted. This era marked the beginning of questioning and slowly redefining gender roles, though progress was gradual.

The media has been instrumental in both reinforcing and challenging gender stereotypes as this has been evident in how media representations of women have evolved to reflect broader societal changes. Early portrayals often showcased women in passive roles, emphasizing beauty and domesticity. However, as women's rights movements gained momentum, media narratives started to include more diverse and empowered female characters. This shift in representation helped broaden the understanding of femininity, showing that it could encompass strength, intelligence, and independence alongside traditional qualities. As we moved into the twentieth century, significant strides were made in gender equality. Women fought for and gained the right to vote, access to education, and better employment opportunities. These achievements began to reshape societal norms and the concept of femininity as women persisted in proving that they could excel in various fields traditionally dominated by men, challenging outdated notions of what it meant to be feminine. However, despite these advances, the battle against deep-seated stereotypes continued.

The feminist movements of the 1960s and 1970s further transformed perceptions of femininity. These movements advocated for women's liberation from restrictive gender roles, promoting the idea that women should have the freedom to choose their paths without societal constraints. Feminists rejected the notion that femininity was inherently tied to passivity or subordination, arguing instead for a broader, more inclusive definition that allowed women to express themselves fully and authentically. Modern-day discussions about gender roles and femininity continue to evolve, recognizing the fluidity and complexity of these concepts. Today's society is more aware of the damaging effects of strict gender binaries and is increasingly embracing diversity in gender expression. This progress is reflected in the push for gender-neutral policies and the celebration of individuals who defy traditional gender norms.

Despite the progress made, challenges remain. Many women still face pressure to conform to traditional standards of femininity, whether in personal relationships, workplaces, or media representations. These pressures can affect self-esteem and limit women's ability to explore their identities fully. Reflecting on historical gender roles helps us understand the long-standing impact of these norms on women's lives. It also highlights the importance of continuing to challenge and redefine these roles to create a more equitable and inclusive society. By acknowledging the complexities of gender and promoting diverse expressions of femininity, we can support women in exploring their full potential, free from the constraints of outdated stereotypes. In examining the evolution of gender roles and their impact on defining femininity, we see a dynamic interplay between tradition and progress. Understanding this history provides valuable insights into the ongoing journey toward gender equality and the redefinition of what it means to be feminine. Each step forward allows women greater freedom to define themselves on their own terms, contributing to a richer, more varied tapestry of human experience.

The role of patriarchy in shaping societal expectations of women

Recognizing the historical context of femininity can help us redefine modern perceptions and expectations of womanhood since femininity has been defined and redefined countless times across various cultures and epochs. When we examine how gender roles have evolved, we gain valuable insights into how societal constructs have shaped and continue to shape our understanding of what it means to be a woman. This exploration is crucial for challenging outdated notions and fostering a more inclusive and authentic expression of womanhood. In early human societies, gender roles were often influenced by practical needs, where men typically hunted while women gathered, cared for children, and maintained the home. These divisions were not strictly based on inherent abilities but rather on the necessities of survival. As societies progressed, these roles became more rigid, morphing into social norms that dictated specific behaviors and responsibilities for men and women. These further developed into entrenched stereotypes, which became difficult to shake off even when they were no longer applicable.

Looking at different cultures highlights that gender roles are not universal truths but socially constructed norms. For instance, in many Native American and African tribes, women historically held significant power as leaders and healers, contrasting sharply with the patriarchal structures of many Asian and European societies where men dominated social and political arenas (Nash 2016). These cultural variations indicate that femininity is not a fixed concept but one that changes depending on time and place. Moreover, examining specific periods in history reveals how flexible and sometimes contradictory these roles can be. Consider the color associations we take for granted today: pink for girls and blue for boys. Joy Nash (2016) further adds that this was not always the case since up until the mid-twentieth century, pink was seen as a strong, masculine color while blue was considered delicate and feminine. The shift in color symbolism serves as a reminder of how arbitrary and changeable gendered attributes can be.

One striking example is the use of high heels. They were originally worn by men in the Middle Ages to signify status and masculinity. It wasn't until later that they became associated exclusively with femininity. This demonstrates that many traits and symbols we currently associate with gender are products of cultural evolution rather than inherent differences between sexes (Nash 2016). As societies industrialized and modernized, the roles of women began to shift again. With the need for labor during wars and the rise of the feminist movement, women started participating more actively in public life, gaining rights, and advocating for equality. Despite these advances, traditional gender roles still persist, often hindering individuals from expressing their true selves. This persistence underscores the importance of recognizing and questioning these historical contexts.

Understanding this fluidity allows us to question the current standards of femininity. If past societies could redefine gender roles, this means that we can still do the same today. Empowering women and young girls to express themselves beyond traditional feminine expectations involves encouraging them to explore their interests and talents freely without the constraints of societal stereotypes. When considering the impact of these evolving roles on modern perceptions, it's essential to recognize that everyone's experience of femininity is unique. The pressure to conform to a narrow set of expectations can be stifling. By acknowledging the diversity of gender expressions throughout history, we validate those who might not fit into conventional molds. Breaking free from these constraints allows for a broader and more inclusive definition of femininity that resonates personally with each individual.

Thus, redefining modern perceptions of womanhood requires us to look back at history and see how these roles have been flexible and varied. Embracing this understanding helps dismantle the limiting stereotypes and opens up a space for every woman to define femininity on her terms. By reflecting on the historical shifts in gender roles, we appreciate the dynamic nature of femininity. This appreciation fosters an environment where all expressions of womanhood are respected and celebrated. It is through this lens that we can build a future where personal identity takes precedence over archaic societal expectations.

Impact of societal expectations on women's self-perception and identity

While femininity may seem like a personal concept, it is greatly influenced by societal pressures and historical ideals. From a young age, women are subtly and not-so-subtly guided toward certain behaviors, appearances, and roles. This internal guidance system often stems from cultural norms and the portrayal of the "ideal woman," which can significantly impact women's self-esteem and self-worth. The ideal image of a woman has changed through centuries, yet it consistently puts tremendous pressure on women to conform. Historically, the Victorian era's corsets or the 1920s flapper style imposed strict body standards. Even today, the media continues to bombard women with images of an idealized form, creating a constant comparison game that affects how they perceive themselves (Ngo 2019). Nealie's 2016 article titled "What Historical Ideals of Women's Shapes Teach Us About Women's Self-Perception and Body Decisions Today" highlighted how body dissatisfaction can lead to poor emotional well-being and disordered eating, ultimately lowering a woman's sense of worth and agency.

One significant point of reflection here is understanding why we, as a society, persist in holding onto such fixed ideals. Is there a way to dismantle these pervasive norms? For many women, realizing their individuality means rejecting the stereotype of the ideal woman. It is essential to teach young girls to value their bodies for what they can do rather than how they appear. By shifting the focus from appearance to capability, we may begin to cultivate healthier self-perceptions among women. Additionally, conversations within families play a pivotal role in shaping body image and femininity since parents' remarks about weight or appearance can leave lasting imprints, knowingly or unknowingly contributing to a daughter's self-consciousness. A study revealed that body image was a significant concern for adolescent girls, ranking third behind stress and academic issues (Ngo 2019). This emphasizes the need for parents to foster discussions around self-worth that go beyond appearance as this will encourage children to appreciate diverse body types and promote a healthy lifestyle rather than aesthetic goals that can be transformative.

Moreover, societal pressures to embody the ideal woman often extend into adulthood, impacting self-esteem and professional success. Women are frequently judged more harshly on their appearances, influencing their confidence and opportunities in various domains. Addressing this, workplaces and communities should celebrate and support diversity in body shapes and sizes. Promoting inclusive beauty standards and challenging derogatory comments about appearance can create a more accepting environment. Lastly, education and media literacy are critical tools in deconstructing harmful stereotypes. By teaching young girls to critically analyze media portrayals and understand the unrealistic nature of many beauty standards, we empower them to form their own identities. Schools and community programs could include workshops on body positivity and self-acceptance, helping to instill values that prioritize well-being over conformity.

The need for evaluating the societal pressures that shape beliefs about femininity is vital in dismantling the concept of the ideal woman. Promoting individuality and self-acceptance through family discussions, supportive environments, and educational initiatives can foster a generation of women who value themselves for who they are, not how they look. It starts with small shifts in conversation and representation, gradually leading to broader societal change. Together, we can move toward a culture where every woman's unique essence is celebrated, laying down the foundation for future generations to thrive without the constraints of outdated ideals.

Linking traditional gender roles and women's sense of identity

Exploring the evolution of gender roles throughout history reveals how powerful societal influences can empower women to redefine femininity on their own terms. This journey is not just a matter of historical curiosity but a path laden with profound implications for our present and future. The 1920s in Paris, a period often romanticized for its artistic flourish and cultural vibrancy, played a crucial role in reshaping traditional female roles. Women like Gertrude Stein, Josephine Baker, and Zelda Fitzgerald embodied this transformation. They transcended the conventional boundaries set by society, showing that women could thrive independently, creatively, and intellectually. These pioneering figures inspired countless others to embrace their identities outside the domestic sphere, moving toward academic, career, and artistic ambitions without relying entirely on male support. Such movements ignited a collective shift in how femininity was perceived (Gonzalez et al. 2022).

Fast forward to the 1990s, another pivotal decade marked by the rise of "girl power." This era saw a surge in media representation of women claiming their space and autonomy. Icons like Britney Spears and the Spice Girls popularized a form of empowerment rooted in self-expression and confidence. However, this notion of empowerment was sometimes co-opted by consumerism, morphing into a message that equated female liberation with sexualization, often to fit market interests. Critical analysis pointed out that such portrayals did not always reflect genuine empowerment but rather perpetuated new forms of objectification (Evans et al. 2022). Understanding these shifts helps us see that terminology like *empowerment* can be multifaceted and, at times, misleading. It underscores the importance of critically examining societal influences to ensure they are genuinely beneficial. For contemporary women looking to define femininity on their own terms, this historical insight offers valuable lessons.

Some of the ways in which we can reclaim and redefine femininity are listed below:

- Reflect on historical examples of strong, independent women who challenged societal norms.
- Critically analyze modern representations of women in the media to distinguish between authentic empowerment and exploitative portrayals.
- Embrace diverse expressions of femininity, acknowledging that there is no single correct way to be a woman.
- Foster supportive communities where women can share their experiences and learn from one another.

Incorporating these actions into daily life can create a more inclusive and empowering environment for women of all backgrounds. As we look back at the challenges and triumphs of those who came before us, we find both inspiration and cautionary tales. Whether it is the intellectual independence showcased by women in the 1920s or the mixed messages of the 1990s girl power movement, each era teaches us something about the ongoing quest for genuine empowerment. It's essential to recognize that while individual efforts are vital, larger systemic changes are also necessary. Policies that address gender disparities in workplaces, education, and healthcare can provide the structural support women need to thrive. Governments and corporations should collaborate with checks and balances to ensure public interests are safeguarded. Empowering women requires both personal responsibility and institutional accountability to foster an environment where everyone has the opportunity to succeed.

Redefining femininity involves encouraging young girls to explore various interests and fields, breaking away from the stereotypes that typically dictate what women should pursue. Education systems play a significant role here by promoting gender-neutral activities and subjects, helping young minds understand that capability and potential have no predetermined gender. By understanding the historical evolution of gender roles and their impact on defining femininity, we are given tools to carve out new paths. By learning from the past, embracing diversity, and pushing for systemic change, we can create a society where women's empowerment is not just a buzzword but a lived reality.

Modern perspectives on embracing diverse forms of femininity

The evolution of gender roles throughout history and how they have shaped our understanding of femininity has been discussed at great length, where the journey from rigid domestic duties to challenging societal norms has been highlighted, and where we've noted how women's roles have changed in many ways. These shifts show that femininity is not a fixed concept but a fluid one, influenced by the times and cultures we live in. We started by looking at how traditional gender roles confined women to the home, expected to be nurturing and gentle. Over time, these stereotypes seeped into women's self-perceptions, shaping their identities from a young age. As society progressed, especially during the industrial revolution and the feminist movements of the 1960s and 1970s, women began to break free from these constraints. They started entering the workforce, fighting for rights, and redefining what it means to be a woman.

The role of media has been both supportive and restrictive. Early portrayals often reinforced passive roles for women, but as women's rights movements gained momentum, more diverse and empowered female characters emerged. This broader representation helped change perceptions of femininity, showing that it could include qualities like strength, intelligence, and independence. Today, discussions about gender roles and femininity continue to evolve. We are more aware of the damaging effects of strict gender binaries and increasingly embrace diverse expressions of gender. Despite this progress, many women still face pressure to conform to traditional standards of femininity, which can affect their self-esteem and limit their ability to explore their identities fully.

By reflecting on these historical contexts, we gain valuable insights into the long-standing impact of gender norms on women's lives. More importantly, it emphasizes the need to keep challenging and redefining these roles to create a fairer and more inclusive society. Understanding the complexities of gender and promoting diverse expressions of femininity allow us to support women in realizing their full potential, free from outdated stereotypes. As we move forward, let's remember that redefining femininity requires both personal efforts and systemic changes. Empowering women involves encouraging them to explore interests and fields beyond traditional expectations freely. By embracing diversity, supporting each other, and pushing for policies that address gender disparities, we can pave the way for future generations to thrive without the constraints of old norms.

So let's continue this journey together, recognizing that the quest for genuine empowerment is ongoing. Each step we take brings us closer to a world where every woman can define herself on her own terms, contributing to a richer and more varied tapestry of human experience.

*****

*The truest beauty that can be witnessed in our society is when we start witnessing **Women Optimizing Mastery And Nobility** in all the endeavors that help them reach greater heights in their lives.*

CHAPTER 4

Resilience and Beyond: Women's Enduring Strength

Women, in their uniqueness, draw strength from the depths of their souls, emerging resilient from the fires of adversity with grace in their hearts and power in their spirits.

Have you ever wondered how some women manage to rise above their toughest challenges and come out even stronger? Their stories of resilience can provide hope and inspiration for all of us. By looking at the journeys of such women, we can learn valuable lessons on facing our own struggles with determination and courage. An example of such a figure is Billie Jean King, a legendary tennis player who not only excelled in her sport but also fought fiercely for gender equality. In 1973, she famously defeated Bobby Riggs in the Battle of the Sexes, proving that women could compete with men on equal footing.

Another inspirational story comes from Simone Biles, an extraordinary gymnast who prioritized her mental health by withdrawing from the 2021 Tokyo Olympics. This bold decision highlighted the importance of mental well-being, showing that true strength involves caring for both mind and body. These examples illustrate that overcoming adversity requires more than physical prowess; it demands mental fortitude and self-belief.

You will get a chance to reflect on real-life stories of women like Billie Jean King and Simone Biles, whose experiences offer insights into how to confront and conquer obstacles. Through their tales of triumph, you will see how they turned setbacks into stepping stones, inspiring us to face our own challenges head-on. By delving into these narratives, my aim is to motivate you to embrace your inner strength and approach life's adversities with renewed confidence and determination.

Women Overcoming Challenges

When we hear stories of women facing adversity and emerging stronger, it can either be incredibly motivating or pressure-inducing although this should be viewed in a positive light. With the two real-life examples that were mentioned, we are shown that no matter how tough the situation may be, there is always a way through it. Let's take Billie Jean King, for example, who is a retired American tennis player who not only excelled on the court but also made significant strides in advocating for gender equality in sports. In 1973, she played against Bobby Riggs, a former tennis champion who believed women's tennis was inferior to men's. Maddie Buher's 2023 article titled "Professional Athletes and How They Have Overcome Challenges—Inspiration for Female Athletes" retraces how the match, dubbed the Battle of the Sexes, ended with Billie Jean King sweeping Riggs in three straight sets. Her victory was a powerful statement against gender stereotypes, proving that women could compete and win against men on an equal playing field.

Buher's article further expands on how King also championed for equal pay for female athletes, fighting the prevalent pay gap in tennis and advocating for fair compensation. Her efforts led to substantial advancements in prize money equality, paving the way for future generations. King's determination and advocacy reshaped societal perceptions, making her a trailblazer in women's sports. On the other hand, Simone Biles, an American gymnast, was known for her extraordinary accomplishments and being the most decorated gymnast in history. In 2021, she took a courageous step by withdrawing from the Tokyo Olympics to focus on her mental health, highlighting the importance of mental well-being in sports (Buher 2023). This move brought significant attention to the pressures athletes face and emphasized that mental health is as crucial as physical fitness.

Biles has been open about her struggles with anxiety and performance pressure, encouraging athletes to prioritize self-care and seek help when needed. Her actions have sparked much-needed conversations about mental health in sports, promoting a more understanding environment for all athletes. By sharing her vulnerabilities, she has empowered others to take their mental health seriously. These incredible women remind us that challenges are opportunities to prove our strength and resilience, where facing adversity doesn't mean you will be defeated; it means you have a chance to rise and show what you are truly capable of. When we see someone like Billie Jean King or Simone Biles pushing boundaries and breaking barriers, it inspires us to tackle our own obstacles with similar courage and tenacity.

In essence, it is not just about reaching the top in your respective field; it is about how you get there. Both King and Biles have shown us that overcoming adversity involves more than physical prowess; it is about mental strength, self-belief, and unyielding advocacy for what's right. Their journeys offer valuable lessons in resilience, reminding us to fight for our place and well-being in whatever arena we find ourselves in. By drawing inspiration from these women, we can confront our own challenges with renewed vigor and confidence.

Understanding personal struggles and inner strength

In Daly et al.'s 2023 article titled "Women's Perspectives on Resilience and Research on Resilience in Motherhood: A Qualitative Study," one woman reflected by mentioning the following, "I don't feel like

I'm more resilient than anybody else: I think I've been able to be resilient because of everything that I have." This highlights how external factors play a crucial role in shaping one's capacity to adapt and overcome.

For many women, the word *coping* has negative connotations, particularly in connection with motherhood. Coping is often seen as barely getting by whereas resilience is viewed as thriving despite challenges. Women believed that focusing solely on coping strategies misses the broader picture of resilience, which involves finding long-term solutions and thriving, not merely surviving. From this standpoint, shifting from just learning to cope to cultivating resilience by identifying and leveraging long-term resources and support systems is essential. Seeking help through friends, family, or professional services creates a network that bolsters one's ability to withstand and grow from adversities.

Reflecting on the journeys of resilient women can inspire women to find their inner strength. One way to do this is by

- identifying role models who exemplify resilience,
- observing how they navigate through hardships,
- applying these observations to one's own life to develop personalized strategies for overcoming obstacles, and
- seeking out community resources that can provide support and encouragement.

Resilience doesn't mean the absence of challenges but rather finding ways to adapt and thrive despite them. Women shared their experiences of mental health coexisting with resilience, stressing that resilience should not be viewed as simply the absence of distress but as the capacity to maintain positive outcomes despite adverse conditions (Daly et al. 2023). In navigating through hardships, resilient women often spoke about maintaining a sense of self and pursuing personal goals, which helps them stay anchored. Creativity and engaging in new hobbies or interests are avenues through which women can nurture a sense of identity outside their roles, supporting social relationships and personal growth.

Women highlighted the importance of viewing resilience research not just as a means to evaluate individual traits but as an intersection of personal, familial, cultural, and social influences. This holistic view ensures that research findings genuinely reflect women's lived experiences and needs. One recurring theme in discussions was that of inclusion and respect in research. Women want future research to center on their voices and experiences, ensuring that it respects their perspectives and provides actionable, compassionate insights into addressing the challenges they face.

Acknowledging the complexities of women's lives and the multifaceted nature of resilience can offer profound insights into developing effective strategies for overcoming obstacles. In understanding that resilience can coexist with mental health challenges, women can recognize their strength and capacity to create positive outcomes despite difficulties. It is important for women to adopt similar practices by

- reaching out for support when needed;
- being open about their challenges without fear of judgment;
- fostering a positive mindset; and
- giving themselves credit for their achievements, however small they may seem.

As societal norms and expectations evolve, there must also be a shift in how resilience is perceived and fostered in women. Both personal responsibility and external support systems are essential in helping women navigate life's inevitable hurdles. By embracing a holistic approach to resilience, women can better equip themselves to handle adversities, emerging stronger and more empowered. Reflecting on the strengths and stories of resilient women can profoundly influence our understanding and application of resilience in our own lives. It is about finding sustainable ways to live fully and joyfully, even amid the storms, by nurturing oneself and leaning on available supports to build a robust foundation for the future.

Journeys of resilient women

Reflecting on resilient women's journeys can help them identify with their experiences and find inspiration in their triumphs. By sharing stories of women who faced adversity with courage, we encourage others to do the same. These women serve as role models, demonstrating that resilience is within reach for all of us. Consider the story of Maya Angelou, who overcame a traumatic childhood to become one of the most influential authors and poets of our time. Her journey was not easy since it was filled with challenges and setbacks, but she faced them head-on and emerged stronger. Through her writing, Maya shared her struggles and triumphs, offering a powerful message of hope and perseverance. Her ability to turn pain into purpose resonates deeply, showing us that we, too, can rise above our difficulties.

Another inspiring example is Malala Yousafzai, who courageously advocated for girls' education in the face of extreme danger. After surviving a life-threatening assassination attempt, Malala's determination only grew more robust as she utilized her experience to amplify her voice and fight for the rights of millions of girls worldwide. Malala's story is a testament to the power of resilience and the impact one person can have when they refuse to be silenced by fear. She went on to become the youngest Nobel Prize laureate in 2014. Learning from other women's experiences helps us develop strategies for overcoming our own obstacles. For instance, Oprah Winfrey's rise from poverty and abuse to become a global media mogul is a profound lesson in resilience and determination. Despite facing numerous barriers, Oprah remained focused on her goals and worked tirelessly to achieve them. Her journey teaches us the importance of perseverance, hard work, and believing in oneself even when the odds seem insurmountable.

Developing resilience also involves recognizing the value of community support. Building relationships that empower us to overcome obstacles is crucial. When we seek and offer support within a community, we enhance both individual resilience and collective strength. Having a network of supportive friends, family, or mentors can provide emotional encouragement and practical assistance during tough times. Strengthening these bonds ensures that no one has to face their challenges alone.

To build a supportive network,

- reach out to people who inspire you and share similar values;
- engage in community activities and join groups that align with your interests and goals;
- offer support to others, creating a reciprocal environment of mutual empowerment; and
- stay connected and communicate regularly to maintain strong relationships.

Finding inspiration in stories of triumph can spark the courage needed to face personal challenges. The stories of women like J. K. Rowling, who wrote the first *Harry Potter* book while struggling as a single mother, demonstrate that persistence pays off. Despite numerous rejections, she continued to write and eventually created one of the most beloved literary franchises in history. Her story reminds us that our current circumstances do not define our future potential.

The resilience displayed by athletes like Serena Williams also offers valuable lessons. Serena faced multiple adversities, including health issues and public scrutiny. Yet her unyielding dedication and mental toughness propelled her to become one of the greatest tennis players of all time. Her journey illustrates the importance of maintaining focus, building inner strength, and continually pushing boundaries. Encouraging women to face challenges with resilience involves more than just telling stories; it requires fostering a mindset that embraces growth. Understand that obstacles are part of the journey and each setback is an opportunity to learn and grow stronger. Reflecting on how resilient women navigated their paths can offer the following practical insights:

- Embrace a positive outlook and believe in your ability to overcome difficulties.
- Set realistic goals and break them down into smaller manageable steps.
- Develop healthy coping mechanisms such as mindfulness, exercise, and creative outlets.
- Learn from past experiences and apply those lessons to new situations.

These stories empower us all to confront our own challenges with courage and determination. We can draw inspiration from their journeys and learn the value of perseverance and the importance of a strong support network. Let these stories remind us that while adversity is inevitable, our response to it defines our strength and character.

As anchors, how are women influential?

In the face of adversity, women have consistently demonstrated incredible resilience. A significant part of this resilience comes from the support of their communities. The power of community cannot be overstated when it comes to nurturing resilience in women. Community support plays a vital role in providing emotional encouragement, resources, and a sense of belonging—all of which are essential for women facing challenges. Communities act as a backbone for women by offering emotional support. When women find themselves amid life's most challenging battles, knowing they have a network of people who genuinely care about their well-being can provide immense comfort. Emotional support from friends, family, and community members helps women feel understood and less isolated, significantly boosting their morale and confidence. This shared empathy strengthens their resolve to overcome obstacles.

Beyond emotional support, communities provide practical resources that can be crucial in times of need. Access to helpful information, financial aid, or even just a platform to share experiences can make a huge difference. For instance, women's empowerment programs often offer educational and vocational training that equips women with skills necessary for economic independence. Programs like those initiated by the Sambhav Foundation have shown tangible improvements in the lives of women by transforming them into active community participants (Foundation 2023). The trials and triumphs of these remarkable women resonate deeply with many, highlighting the strength and resilience that lie within each of us. Hearing their stories can ignite a spark within, motivating us to face our own challenges head-on. Through their experiences, we find solace in knowing we are not alone in our struggles.

Remembering the journey of astronaut Dr. Mae Jemison, who shattered barriers as the first African American woman to travel to space, is a testament to her unwavering determination. Despite facing naysayers and obstacles, she pursued her dream relentlessly. Dr. Jemison's story empowers us to reach for the stars, emphasizing the importance of breaking boundaries and embracing one's uniqueness. Taking a page from the life of Wangari Maathai, the renowned environmentalist and Nobel Peace Prize laureate, reveals the resilience born from a deep-rooted passion for the planet. Her Green Belt Movement, established in 1977, focused on conservation and women's empowerment and showcased the impact of grassroots efforts in fostering positive change. Maathai's legacy reinforces the notion that small actions can lead to significant transformations.

Delving into the world of music, the journey of Adele, a chart-topping artist known for her soulful voice and heartfelt lyrics, evokes feelings of empowerment and vulnerability. Through her music, Adele opens her heart to her listeners, sharing tales of love, heartbreak, and self-discovery. Her ability to connect with audiences profoundly and emotionally underscores the power of authenticity and raw expression. An often-overlooked story of resilience lies in the everyday heroes around us. Consider the working mother juggling career demands and family responsibilities, persevering through long hours and sleepless nights with unwavering dedication. Her resilience shines through in the face of adversity, serving as a silent but potent inspiration to those who witness her tireless efforts.

In a world where challenges abound, drawing strength from the narratives of resilient women offers a beacon of hope and guidance. Their journeys remind us of the boundless potential within each individual to overcome obstacles, embrace growth, and emerge more vital than ever before. When a woman knows she has a supportive network, she gains the confidence to tackle her problems head-on. Strong interpersonal relationships within her community foster a sense of security and belonging. Women who engage in communal activities and build connections tend to show greater resilience because they know they're not alone in their struggles. These relationships empower them to take risks and pursue solutions they might otherwise avoid. Some of the ways to cultivate a supportive network include the following steps:

- Start by reaching out to local organizations or groups that focus on women's empowerment. Getting involved in community initiatives is a great way to meet like-minded individuals.
- Build and maintain close ties with friends and family who can offer emotional and practical support.
- Participate in workshops, seminars, and social events that align with your interests. Engaging in such activities helps to form new connections and strengthen existing ones.
- Offer your own support to others. Supporting fellow women in their endeavors creates a reciprocal relationship that benefits everyone involved.

Moreover, leveraging communal resources for personal growth is key to enhancing individual resilience. Women who tap into community-based programs often find opportunities they might not have discovered on their own. For example, accessing health services through community health initiatives ensures that women stay healthy and capable of handling life's demands. Informal networks can provide an excellent framework for guidance and assistance in areas where formal support systems may be lacking. The significance of fostering relationships within a community extends beyond personal benefits. Offering and seeking support cultivates collective strength. When women work together, they create a powerful force capable of driving change and improving overall community welfare. This mutual empowerment enhances individual resilience and results in a more robust, supportive community.

By recognizing the value of community support and actively participating in building these networks, women can better navigate adversities and thrive. Whether through formal programs or informal connections, coming together to share resources, offer encouragement, and provide a listening ear profoundly impacts resilience. It fosters a culture where women uplift one another, ensuring no one faces their challenges alone. As we reflect on the importance of community, it is evident that solid community ties foster resilience in women. Understanding and utilizing the collective power of a supportive network can transform challenges into stepping stones toward greater strength and determination. The efforts of involvement, connection, and mutual support lay the foundation for a resilient, thriving community where women can emerge stronger than ever before.

Psychological aspects of resilience and empowerment

Throughout this chapter, we've explored some formidable examples of women who faced adversity head-on and emerged stronger. By sharing the journeys of figures like Billie Jean King and Simone Biles, we've shed light on how challenges can be transformed into opportunities for growth and strength. Their stories are not just about victories in sports; they reveal deep-seated lessons in resilience, mental fortitude, and advocacy for what is right. By reflecting on these narratives, we see a common theme of facing seemingly insurmountable obstacles with courage and determination. These women inspire us to look at our challenges not as blockades but as chances to rise and prove our capabilities. Just as King challenged gender stereotypes on the tennis court and Biles brought crucial attention to mental health in sports, we too can confront our struggles with similar resilience.

Resilience and empowerment in women are closely tied to various psychological aspects. One crucial factor is the role of self-belief and confidence in fostering resilience. Believing in oneself can significantly impact how women navigate challenges and setbacks. Confidence protects against self-doubt and fear, empowering women to face difficulties with a positive outlook. Moreover, trusting in their capabilities enables women to persevere in the face of adversity and bounce back stronger. Embracing one's strengths and talents is key to cultivating resilience and empowerment, showcasing the power of a strong self-belief system as a driving force for women's success and endurance.

What's noteworthy is that resilience is not an inherent trait limited to a few; it is something we can all cultivate. The stories we've discussed underline the importance of support systems, whether that's community networks, family, or friends. They remind us that seeking help is a sign of strength, not weakness. For many young girls and women, understanding that resilience involves more than coping—it's about thriving despite hardships—is essential. It's easy to feel overwhelmed when faced with tough situations, but knowing that others have navigated similar paths successfully offers hope and guidance. Developing resilience means setting realistic goals, embracing a positive mindset, and harnessing both internal and external resources to bolster one's journey.

On a broader scale, the influence of resilient women extends beyond personal victories. Their actions can shift societal perceptions and create lasting change. When women push back against barriers and advocate for equality and mental health awareness, they pave the way for future generations to encounter fewer obstacles. As you reflect on these extraordinary journeys, consider how their lessons can apply to your own life. Acknowledge the power of resilience within you and the potential to transform adversity into strength. Remember, facing challenges head-on with the support of your community can lead to remarkable personal growth and collective empowerment. So as you move forward, let these stories encourage you to tackle your obstacles with renewed vigor, knowing that resilience is a journey we all can embark on together.

*****

*When observing a women's resilience, you get to witness a **W**himsical **O**bserver **M**aking **A**stute **N**otations, as she will not witness what is within her reach, but she bears the foresight of seeing into what she desires and how best to attain this.*

Chapter 5

Empowerment in the Twenty-First Century

Empowered women continue to be inspired by the voices of courage and change that echo in our history. By continuously redefining the landscape of the twenty-first century with their resilience, they have paved a way to encourage other women's determination to carry the course of equity forward in our societies.

When we start to explore the evolving roles and opportunities for women in contemporary society, it is inevitable that we will not reflect on the challenges they have encountered in the past that still persist in the present day. However, the view within the contemporary scope needs to be an optimistic one that not only focuses on what hasn't been going right for women but how this can be remedied for present and future generations. Imagine a world where every woman can pursue her dreams without facing obstacles just because of her gender. This vision is becoming closer to reality as women today have more opportunities than ever before. Education plays a crucial role in this progress as it offers the tools and confidence needed to break through societal barriers. Through learning, women are not only acquiring knowledge but also embracing self-care, self-love, and self-acceptance; and each of these are key elements for personal and professional empowerment.

Despite the strides that have been made, there are still significant challenges that women confront daily since traditional norms and stereotypes often limit women's roles by confining them to certain professions and positions. Look at how many young girls are dissuaded from pursuing careers in science or leadership due to these ingrained biases. Moreover, financial constraints and a lack of supportive environments can disproportionately affect girls' access to quality education. These barriers prevent many women from realizing their full potential, perpetuating cycles of inequality and limiting overall societal progress.

This chapter will delve into how education fosters a sense of self-worth and independence among women while equipping them with the necessary skills to navigate life's complexities. It'll further explore the importance of self-acceptance, self-care, and self-love learned through educational experiences. By analyzing real-world examples and highlighting successful initiatives, we will see how these elements empower women to challenge the status quo and build fulfilling lives. This understanding is vital in creating a more equitable society where everyone has the opportunity to thrive.

Education and Empowerment

Education provides the necessary knowledge, skills, and curiosity to assert yourself in various domains, as it helps with fostering independence and an open mind. This is the type of foundation that allows women to build their self-esteem and embrace their identities fully. You will find that when women are educated, they also learn about the need to recognize their worth and potential without any limitations hindering them. Having access to education also opens up avenues for women to pursue careers and leadership roles that they would otherwise be told they can't assume, and this is an ongoing effort to break traditional barriers imposed by societal norms.

As we start seeing more women stepping into these roles, they serve as role models and demonstrate that gender should never be a limiting factor in achieving any aspirations you might have. Think about this: When women are given the opportunity to learn, they gain the tools to question and challenge the norms that have held them back. They start to understand their rights and how to advocate for themselves and others as well. Through quality education, skills such as critical thinking and problem-solving are also fostered, enabling women to navigate complex situations with more confidence. This is incredibly powerful as it means that women can take control of their lives and contribute meaningfully to their communities and society at large.

Through the promotion of self-love, education encourages women to appreciate and celebrate their unique qualities while also teaching them to prioritize their well-being by understanding that caring for themselves is not selfish but essential. Through self-care practices that are learned via education, women can maintain their physical and mental health, which is vital for long-term success and happiness. Having knowledge about personal health, hygiene, and wellness equips women with making informed decisions about their bodies and lifestyles.

Self-acceptance is another crucial element fostered through education as it helps women acknowledge and embrace their strengths and weaknesses without judgment. Recognizing one's individuality and being proud of it can lead to a more fulfilling and authentic life. In educational settings, women are encouraged to explore different aspects of their personalities and interests, providing a holistic approach to personal development. This holistic approach can often include mentorship programs, workshops, and peer support groups that create a nurturing environment for growth.

Moreover, education's impact on career opportunities cannot be overstated. Educated women have higher chances of securing well-paying jobs, moving upward in their professions, and attaining leadership positions. This economic empowerment not only benefits individuals but also has a ripple effect on families and communities. Financial independence allows women to make decisions that align with their values and goals, further reinforcing their sense of autonomy and self-worth. Yet it is important to remember that the journey toward empowerment through education is not always straightforward. Challenges such as financial constraints, cultural norms, and limited access to resources can impede women's educational paths.

Here are a few ways that these issues can be addressed:

- Provide scholarships and financial aid specifically targeted at women and girls from economically disadvantaged backgrounds.
- Create safe and supportive learning environments where women feel valued and respected.
- Advocate for policies that ensure equal access to education for all women, regardless of their socioeconomic status or location.
- Develop community programs that raise awareness about the importance of educating women and encourage families to prioritize their daughters' education.

By focusing on these areas, we can help more women overcome obstacles and take full advantage of educational opportunities. It needs to be emphasized how education is a very transformative process that enables women to discover their potential and assert their place in society. It equips them with the knowledge and skills needed to thrive in various domains. Through the promotion of self-love, self-care, and self-acceptance, education empowers women to lead fulfilling lives and contribute meaningfully to their communities. As we continue to break down barriers and expand access to education, the world will undoubtedly become a more equitable and inclusive place for everyone.

Challenging Societal Norms

Empowering women through education is not just a noble goal; it is essential for driving social progress and creating equitable communities. Educated women are better equipped to assert their rights and navigate life with resilience and determination. One crucial aspect of education for women is promoting self-love. In many societies, women are bombarded with unrealistic standards of beauty and behavior, and education challenges these harmful stereotypes by providing women with the knowledge to appreciate the traits that make them unique. Schools can incorporate programs that focus on body positivity and mental health, helping girls and women see themselves through a lens of appreciation rather than criticism.

Consider a story about how schools around a remote village began implementing programs in response to the alarming rates of low self-esteem and mental health issues among their female students. During one of these sessions, a young girl named Lily found herself captivated by the idea of embracing her imperfections and loving herself as she was. Lily had always struggled with her body image, constantly comparing herself to her classmates and the unrealistic standards set by social media. But as she listened to the speakers and engaged in the activities, something inside her began to shift. She started to see her worth beyond her appearance and realized that true beauty comes from within.

The impact of these programs extended far beyond just boosting self-confidence. It sparked a ripple effect in the student body, leading to more inclusive and supportive environments within the school. Girls were seen standing up for one another, offering words of encouragement, and celebrating each other's achievements. The culture of competition and comparison slowly faded, making room for collaboration and empowerment. Teachers noticed a positive change in the overall dynamics of the classes, with students more willing to participate and express themselves freely.

As the weeks went by, Lily became a beacon of positivity in her school. Her newfound confidence inspired others to embrace themselves and spread kindness wherever they went. One day, during their lunch break, Lily noticed a group of girls whispering and giggling in a corner. Approaching them, she heard snippets of a conversation that made her heart sink. They were making fun of a classmate's outfit, criticizing her choice, and laughing at her. Without hesitation, Lily took a deep breath and approached the group, her voice remaining firm but gentle as she addressed their behavior. She reminded them of the importance of kindness and understanding, urging them to consider how their words could hurt others. To her surprise, the girls listened, their expressions softening as they realized the impact of their words.

The encounter spread like wildfire throughout the school, becoming a powerful example of the change that was taking place within the student community. Lily's courage resonated with others, prompting many to reflect on their own actions and attitudes. More girls started speaking out against bullying and negativity, and they were choosing to uplift and support one another instead. The hallways that were once toxic transformed into spaces filled with laughter and camaraderie, a testament to the power of self-love and acceptance.

With each passing day, the school became a sanctuary for girls to learn, grow, and thrive in an environment that celebrated their individuality. The programs on body positivity and mental health became a cornerstone of the school's curriculum, fostering a culture of empowerment and resilience among the students. Lily's journey from self-doubt to self-love inspired countless others to embark on their path toward acceptance and exercising more care.

Self-care is another critical component of women's education. From a young age, girls should learn the importance of taking care of their physical and mental well-being. This can be integrated into school curricula through classes on nutrition, exercise, stress management, and emotional intelligence. By prioritizing self-care, women can better handle the pressures of everyday life and maintain a balanced lifestyle.

Self-acceptance is intertwined with both self-love and self-care as it means recognizing one's strengths and weaknesses without undue judgment. Education systems can promote self-acceptance by fostering inclusive environments where diversity is celebrated. When girls see role models who look like them (as with Lily's story) and hear stories of women overcoming similar challenges, they are more likely to accept and value their own experiences.

Empowering women through education also has far-reaching benefits for communities. Educated women are more likely to participate in the workforce, leading to economic growth and stability. They are also better positioned to make informed decisions about their health and the well-being of their families. This ripple effect can drive progress in areas such as health care, housing, and education.

Incorporating gender-sensitive policies within educational institutions is vital. Schools should ensure that girls have access to the same resources and opportunities as boys. This includes everything from adequate learning materials to safe and supportive learning environments. Teachers play a critical role and must be trained to recognize and counteract gender biases in the classroom. Communities also have a responsibility to support girls' education by challenging cultural norms that may hinder their progress. In some areas, traditional beliefs still prioritize boys' education over girls'. Community leaders can combat these practices by advocating for the benefits of educating girls and demonstrating how this leads to overall community improvement.

Economic barriers are a significant hurdle for many girls seeking education, and providing scholarships and financial aid to those in need can make a substantial difference. Additionally, investing in infrastructure, such as building more schools in remote areas and ensuring safe transportation, can remove some of the logistical obstacles girls face. Awareness campaigns are powerful tools in shifting perceptions about girls' education since highlighting success stories of women who have achieved great things through education can inspire others. These campaigns can be run through various media—including social networks, local radio, and community events—to reach a broad audience.

For an education system to be truly empowering, it needs to be inclusive. This means adapting teaching methods to cater to different learning styles and needs. Ensuring that girls with disabilities have access to quality education is part of this inclusivity. Schools should provide necessary accommodations and resources to support every student's learning journey. Creating spaces for girls to express themselves and develop leadership skills is also essential, where extracurricular activities such as debate clubs, science fairs, and sports teams can help build confidence and encourage girls to pursue their interests passionately. These activities teach teamwork, problem-solving, and perseverance—skills valuable both within and outside of the classroom.

It is important to note that supporting women while they navigate challenges doesn't end with formal education. Mentoring programs connect young women with experienced professionals who can offer guidance and support. These relationships provide a network of encouragement and practical advice, helping women advance in their chosen fields. Organizations and governments must work together to create policies that support women's education and empowerment. This collaboration should involve setting clear goals, allocating sufficient resources, and consistently monitoring progress. Public accountability and transparency can ensure that these efforts genuinely benefit the intended recipients.

The transformative nature of education for women enables them to love themselves, care for themselves, and accept themselves fully. The development of inclusive and supportive educational frameworks is the cornerstone of laying a foundation for empowering women to break free from societal constraints, continuously improve their lives, and contribute meaningfully to their communities. Fostering an environment where women can thrive academically, emotionally, and socially is undoubtedly a step toward a more just and progressive world.

Resilience through Education

Education is, without a doubt, one of the most powerful tools for empowering everyone. When girls receive a quality education that promotes self-love, self-care, and self-acceptance, it does more than just provide them with academic knowledge. It builds a foundation for them to navigate a rapidly changing world with resilience and determination. Education not only helps them understand their inherent worth, but they also get to navigate through the world with other women who share different or sometimes similar experiences. Self-love and self-acceptance are crucial aspects of any individual's development, and for young girls, these attributes can be life-changing. By teaching girls to value themselves and recognize their capabilities, we are instilling in them the courage to pursue their dreams vigorously. School does play an essential role in promoting these values through inclusive curricula and supportive environments that celebrate diverse identities and talents. This approach not only benefits individual girls but sets a precedent for future generations, encouraging a cycle of empowered women who uplift one another.

However, the current global landscape shows clear gaps in the accessibility and completion rates of education for girls. According to a 2022 article by the World Bank titled "Girls' Education," there are approximately 129 million girls around the world who are out of school, including thirty-two million who are of primary school age and ninety-seven million who are of secondary school age. While primary and secondary school enrollment rates are nearly equal for boys and girls globally, completion rates for girls are significantly lower, especially in low-income countries where only 63 percent of female primary school students finish primary school compared to 67 percent of males (The World Bank 2022). Addressing this issue requires concerted efforts from governments, communities, and international organizations.

Promoting self-care among young girls through education is equally important. When girls learn about physical, emotional, and mental well-being, they are better equipped to take care of themselves and make informed decisions about their lives. Curriculums should include comprehensive health education that covers nutrition, personal hygiene, mental health, and the importance of regular exercise. Providing safe spaces within schools where girls can access this information and seek help without fear of judgment or stigma is vital for fostering a culture of self-care.

The journey toward self-acceptance can be particularly challenging for girls due to societal pressures and unrealistic beauty standards. Teachers and school programs can counteract these pressures by highlighting stories of diverse female role models and offering activities that allow girls to explore and celebrate their unique identities. Encouraging positive body image, dismantling gender stereotypes, and highlighting the strengths of various cultural backgrounds are all ways education can nurture self-acceptance. In many regions, the challenges faced by girls extend beyond the school walls. Issues such as poverty, gender-based violence, early marriage, and adolescent pregnancies often hinder their educational pursuits. Studies show that approximately sixty million girls are sexually assaulted on their way to or at school each year, which has serious consequences for their mental and physical health, leading to lower attendance and higher dropout rates (The World Bank 2022).

Ending school-related gender-based violence must be a priority. Schools should be safe havens where girls can learn without fear. Community and school-level interventions—such as engaging teachers and students in reducing gender-based violence and ensuring effective mechanisms for reporting such incidents—are crucial. Building separate sanitary toilets for girls and introducing gender sensitivity training for teachers can also create safer and more inclusive learning environments. Furthermore, girls who marry young often drop out of school and complete fewer years of education. Ending child marriage through community awareness campaigns and legislative measures can significantly improve girls' educational attainment and potential earnings. Such steps would help break the cycle of poverty and empower young women to contribute effectively to their communities.

From an economic perspective, investing in girls' education yields substantial returns. Better educated women tend to have healthier families, marry later, and participate more actively in the labor market. They are also more likely to advocate for the education of their own children, creating a positive ripple effect across generations. Therefore, ensuring that every girl receives a quality education is not just a moral imperative but also a strategic investment in the future of societies worldwide. The pivotal role that education plays in empowering women by promoting self-love, self-care, and self-acceptance cannot be stressed enough as achieving these goals requires a multifaceted approach that involves curricular changes or adaptability, safe and inclusive school environments, robust community support, and strong legal frameworks. The pursuit of closing the educational gaps and addressing systemic challenges requires us to be mindful that educating a girl means empowering a nation. It is only through sustained collaborative efforts that we can ensure all girls have the opportunity to realize their full potential.

Confronting Challenges in Male-Dominated Fields

Understanding how education plays a crucial role in empowering women and shaping their opportunities in society through the promotion of self-love, self-care, and self-acceptance is fundamental. Women encounter systemic biases and stereotypes in male-dominated industries that hinder their progress and recognition. Despite significant strides over recent years, many organizations still fall short in promoting inclusivity and diversity to create a level playing field for women in leadership and professional spheres. Breaking through the glass ceiling necessitates women asserting their capabilities and challenging ingrained gender norms. It's about advocating for equal opportunities consistently and confidently. Supporting and mentoring programs are invaluable in empowering women to navigate these challenges. Such initiatives help women build networks and advance their careers effectively. By connecting with experienced mentors, women can gain insights and strategies to succeed in environments that demand resilience and advocacy.

The wage and opportunity gaps between men and women are particularly pronounced within any given occupation. Studies conducted through the 2007 US Census Bureau have shown that men typically earn higher wages than women in the same roles. Moreover, research indicates that this disparity is often due to personal biases from organizational decision-makers who tend to offer men higher starting salaries (Steinpreis et al. 1999, Moss-Racusin et al. 2012). Acknowledging this reality is a crucial step in addressing the obstacles women face in the workplace. Discrimination in HR policies and practices also plays a role, with biased decisions negatively affecting women's pay and opportunities at work (Son Hing and Starmarski 2015). Additionally, gender harassment during HR processes and outcomes further exacerbates this issue, making it imperative for organizations to recognize and address these biases (Fitzgerald et al. 1995 a, b).

Organizational structures and cultures significantly influence gender equality. For instance, women are underrepresented in leadership positions, and this lack of representation perpetuates gender discrimination within organizations (Konrad et al. 2010). The presence of women in key roles signals an organization's commitment to gender diversity, which can help reduce these inequalities. Job ladders within organizations often remain segregated by gender, limiting women's access to information, status, and upward mobility (Ragins and Sundstrom 1989). To address this, organizations need to ensure that their formal structures support gender integration and equity, providing equal opportunities for all employees to advance.

Addressing gender bias requires conscious efforts from business leaders. Expanding childcare and paid family leave can alleviate some burdens on working women, enabling them to pursue career advancement without sacrificing their personal obligations. Policies such as paid sick days, comprehensive medical leave, and accessible childcare services can make a substantial difference in supporting female employees (St. Catherine University 2022). Additionally, ongoing diversity, inclusion, and equity training is essential. These programs shouldn't be one-off sessions but consistent, reinforced initiatives that challenge deep-seated biases against women in business. Effective training should include practical steps, such as reminding managers about potential biases before conducting employee evaluations.

Women's transformational journey in the digital age is momentous, paving the way for new opportunities and avenues for empowerment. The advancements in technology have not only broken geographic barriers but also fostered a platform for women in diplomacy to amplify their voices globally. As women harness the power of digital tools and social media, they are not only influencing policies but also shaping narratives and fostering connections across borders. Embracing the digital landscape has enabled women to forge impactful relationships, share experiences, and advocate for change in ways that were once unimaginable. As June 24 marks the International Day of Women in Diplomacy, we witness a shift that symbolizes a new chapter in the story of women in diplomacy, one where digital platforms serve as springboards for empowerment and progress.

Finally, embracing digital advocacy tools and platforms can revolutionize the fight for gender equality, engaging women in shaping a more empowered and connected society. Enhancing digital literacy and access for women can bridge the gender gap in technology, employment, and decision-making spaces. Education provides the foundation for women to promote self-love, self-care, and self-acceptance, which are all essential elements for breaking traditional barriers and achieving equal participation and success in male-dominated fields. Supportive environments, conscious policy changes, and inclusive practices are all crucial components in creating a world where women can thrive both personally and professionally.

Advocacy for Gender Equality in the Digital Age and Leveraging Technology for Empowerment

We've explored how education empowers women by fostering self-love, self-care, and self-acceptance. It is about more than just academic knowledge; it is about building confidence and independence. Through education, women can break barriers, challenge societal norms, and pursue careers in any field they choose. Education is not just about learning facts; it is about learning to value oneself. When women understand their worth, they are more likely to take care of both their physical and mental health. This foundation of self-care is vital for long-term happiness and success. Women who practice self-care are better equipped to handle life's challenges, making them stronger and more resilient.

Self-acceptance is another key element. Recognizing and embracing one's strengths and weaknesses without judgment leads to a more fulfilling life. Educational environments that celebrate diversity help women accept and love themselves, paving the way for personal growth and authentic living. However, the path to empowerment through education is not always easy. Many women face financial constraints, cultural norms, and limited access to resources. Addressing these challenges is crucial. Providing scholarships, creating supportive learning environments, and advocating for equal access to education are steps we must take.

The broader consequences of empowering women through education are profound. Educated women are more likely to secure well-paying jobs, achieve leadership positions, and influence future generations positively. Financial independence allows them to make decisions aligned with their values, further enhancing their sense of autonomy and self-worth. Yet even as progress is made, there's still work to be done. Society must continue to support and uplift women, ensuring they have the tools needed to thrive. As we break down educational barriers, we contribute to a more equitable and inclusive world.

Imagine a future where every woman has the opportunity to discover her potential and contribute meaningfully to society. The journey toward that future starts with education—empowering women to live, learn, and lead with confidence. In this future world, young girls will grow up knowing that their dreams and aspirations are valid and that they are supported every step of the way to pursue them. They are encouraged to speak up, to be creative, and to strive for their goals without limitations. As a result, they blossom into strong, empathetic individuals who understand the value of diversity and inclusion, and this shapes a society where everyone is valued and respected for who they are.

*****

*By learning to become a **Warrior Over Mindfulness**,
Ambitiousness, and **Nobility**, you learn to not
only pioneer through challenges you encounter,
but you inadvertently teach those around you
to learn to do the same for themselves.*

CONCLUSION

The journey of women's empowerment is a testament to resilience and determination, from ancient heroines to present-day trailblazers. Throughout history, women have transformed significant challenges into opportunities for growth, relying on community support and personal empowerment. Their stories inspire us to continue advocating for equality, recognizing that progress requires the collective strength of resilience, continuous community engagement, and self-belief. By honoring the past and empowering the present, we pave the way for a more inclusive and equitable future where every individual has the opportunity to thrive.

The Strength of a Woman is aimed at encouraging women to recognize their true power as a birthright bestowed upon them that cannot be taken away by anyone. Throughout the chapters you have read, resilience and empowerment have been the key themes by drawing on personal narratives and societal challenges. Historical perceptions of women, the need for women to embrace their inner strength and advocate for a more balanced society, were explored, along with the biblical portrayals of women, societal norms, barriers hindering their progress, and the importance of self-empowerment for women in the twenty-first century. The systemic barriers faced by women—such as unequal pay, limited access to education and healthcare, gender stereotypes, the need to recognize women's voices, and the dismantling of obstacles that hinder women's progress—are key aspects for the advancement of women that have been highlighted.

Overview of What Was Covered

The focus of this book has been on the historical views of women, their struggles from oppression to liberation, and how societal norms and misconceptions have shaped gender roles, with an emphasis on the importance of advocating for opportunities that empower women. The biblical stories of Esther, Ruth, and Deborah were analyzed to showcase the nurturing and assertive roles women play, along with strategies for empowerment, self-reflection, and self-care to help women embrace their worth. In the same way, women are portrayed as being easily shaken by the challenges they encounter, and inspiration can be derived from how they continue to rise above them. The ideas of how women and men are viewed were also discussed so that a new perspective can be developed to be more inclusive and equal.

Having shared my personal story in the introduction, I highlighted the importance of creating avenues for women to improve their lives by sharing my journey as a mother, wife, doctor, entrepreneur, and an advocate for the motivation of young girls. This was my way of showing every reader that you are strong and capable of anything you set your mind to. Even with the impact of biblical stories still affecting how women are seen today, it is important that more women share their stories of finding their feet in the world. This has given women a chance to understand that when any barrier prevents them from moving forward—such as not getting paid equally, not having the same chances for education and healthcare, not being seen as leaders, and still being judged based on old ideas—it should be their prerogative to trump these views by taking charge of their lives. By becoming aware of what you want and taking care of yourself, you will begin to see your value, what you can do, and how you can make a difference in the world.

The journey for empowering women and advocating for gender equality has proven to be a tough and lengthy one although women continue to work hard to make themselves stronger by setting personal goals, thinking about their future, and taking care of their healthcare needs. Throughout history, women who went against the usual rules and current movements that support equal rights have always fought to find their place in society; and this fight persists despite women being judged based on gender, race, and social status. The importance of resources and education to support inclusivity and understanding in communities was also emphasized, where the promotion of acceptance should be aimed at boosting women's success and confidence. It is necessary to note that inclusive spaces require the recognition and addressing of any discomfort and unfairness to ensure that everyone works together to change this narrative. The mention of the intersectionality between gender, race, and class helped us see that past feminist movements often didn't consider the difficulties faced by women of color and those from poorer backgrounds, which led to a lack of proper support for all. The emphasis further extended to the importance of actively working to address these intersections to create fair policies and environments since developing an understanding of how gender, race, and class are connected helps promote diversity in all areas of life to achieve real gender equality.

The transformation that femininity has undergone over time has altered social expectations and influenced how women are seen in society. Traditional ideas have limited women to certain roles and behaviors, affecting how they view themselves. Feminism today stresses the importance of moving away from these stereotypes and accepting different forms of femininity to create a fairer society. By looking at past changes in gender norms, this will help people better understand gender complexities and support a variety of femininity expressions. The key elements for women to become strong are understanding their personal challenges, having inner strength, and having support from others.

When recalling the stories of women like Billie Jean King, Simone Biles, Maya Angelou, and

Malala Yousafzai, we are shown how overcoming tough times involves mental strength, believing in yourself, and standing up for what's right. You can learn important lessons about being strong in tough situations and the vitality of fighting for your place and well-being in any situation from each of their stories. When women have role models and support from their communities, they become more creative, have a holistic view, and have heightened willpower. By moving away from short-term coping methods to building strong support systems for a long time, women can be inspired to learn and apply these lessons in their everyday lives.

The importance of helping girls succeed in school by making sure they have the right resources and the necessary support needs to be prioritized by all. The promotion of activities such as debate clubs, sports teams, and science fairs is helpful for girls to feel more confident and follow their interests. These activities not only teach them skills such as teamwork and problem-solving but also help girls become leaders. Educational support doesn't only extend to girls within the school environment; those who pursue further educational studies require as much support as possible since we still find that a lot of young women are the first university students in their families, and this results in added pressure being placed on them to excel academically. Professional and career guidance is imperative for young girls and women, where collaborations can be fostered between organizations and the government to develop policies that support women's education at all levels. Accountability and transparency are necessary for the sustainability of these collaborations as this will also curb high drop-out rates, gender-based violence, and early marriages and offer them safe educational environments.

Empowerment in women's daily lives

From ancient heroines to present-day trailblazers, the history of women and how far they have come to be fully recognized as equal contributors in society is a testament of their tenacity and resilience. We owe much to those who walked before us, whose sacrifices have paved the way for current advancements. Understanding this historical context enriches our appreciation of contemporary struggles and achievements, reminding us that change is possible and impactful, irrespective of how long it might take to achieve it. As we look ahead, it is necessary to uphold the balance between economic growth and human welfare. Personal responsibility and robust support systems will ensure that everyone, regardless of gender, can flourish. By embracing diverse perspectives and empirical evidence, we are guided toward policies and practices that genuinely reflect the needs and aspirations of all individuals.

Women can not only relate to this book's content by drawing inspiration from the journeys of resilient women in overcoming societal challenges and striving for empowerment, but they can also establish how they can adapt this in their lives. By reflecting on historical struggles and achievements, women can develop strength in finding their voices and learning how to effectively make these heard so they can extend beyond their immediate environments. The emphasis on self-empowerment, self-reflection, and self-care serves as a guide for women to navigate their daily lives with courage and determination without any self-doubt setting in. I trust that by having read this book, the powerful message that has been shared in relation to the message of resilience, empowerment, and the importance of advocating for gender equality has resonated with you.

I am confident that more women will embrace their inner strength and pursue their aspirations with determination. By continuing to honor the legacy of the courageous women who came before us, we empower future generations to build upon this foundation so they can strive for a world where equality and opportunity are realities for all. Not only will this be a world in which women can become active participants, but they will equally shape the narrative for future generations to better navigate the course of living in a world where equality needs to be embraced across all genders, races, and social classes.

*****

*Encountering a resilient and empowered women is symbolic of meeting a **Wise Oracle Mastering Ambition, and Nobility,** whose strength cannot be measured through their physical might but by the power of their words, actions, and strong will.*

REFERENCES

Aadland, I. 2022. "Casting Biblical Narratives." *Studia Theologica—Nordic Journal of Theology* 77 (1): 40–61. https://doi.org/10.1080/00393 38X.2022.2075461.

Anda, D., J. Eyers, S. Grant, M. Kupfer, L. Langer, E. Lwamba, P. Nduku, W. Ridlehoover, S. Shisler, B. Snilstveit, A. Sonnenfeld, and N. Tshabalala. 2022. "Strengthening Women's Empowerment and Gender Equality in Fragile Contexts towards Peaceful and Inclusive Societies: A Systematic Review and Meta-Analysis." *Campbell Systematic Reviews.* https://www.ncbi. nlm.nih.gov/pmc/articles/PMC8904729/.

BibleGateway.com. n.d. "A Searchable Online Bible in Over 150 Versions and 50 Languages." https://www.biblegateway.com/.

Bioneers. 2020. "Gender Inclusivity and the Importance of Community Support." https:// bioneers.org/gender-inclusivity-and-the-impor-tance-of-community-support/.

Buher, M. 2023. "Professional Athletes and How They Have Overcome Challenges—Inspiration for Female Athletes. Stevenson University. https://

www.stevenson.edu/student-life/health-wellness/blog-news-events/professional-athletes-and-how-they-have-overcome-challenges-inspiration-for-female-athletes/.

Burkett, E. 2024. "Women's Rights Movement." *Encyclopedia Britannica.* https://www.britannica.com/event/womens-movement.

Carson, C. 2024. "American Civil Rights Movement." *Encyclopedia Britannica.* https://www.britannica.com/event/American-civil-rights-movement.

College of Arts and Sciences. n.d. "Intersectionality." https://cas.gsu.edu/advance/intersectionality/.

Daly, D., S. Hannon, and A. Higgins. 2023. "Women's Perspectives on Resilience and Research on Resilience in Motherhood: A Qualitative Study." *Health Expectations.* https://www.ncbi.nlm.nih.gov/pmc/articles/PMC10349245/.

Dearing, H. 2021. "Achievers and Believers: Women Overcoming Obstacles in Business." *Honors Theses.* https://scholarlycommons.obu.edu/honors_theses/803/.

Denova, R. 2021. "Ancient Christianity's Effect on Society and Gender Roles." *World History Encyclopedia.* https://www.worldhistory.org/article/1670/ancient-christianitys-effect-on-society--gender-ro/.

Evans, H., and K. Mooney. 2022. "Researching 1990s feminism in the U.S.: What is Girl Power? An Interview with Hope Evans and Dr. Katherine Mooney | Department of History." history.fsu.edu. https://history.fsu.edu/article/researching-

1990s-feminism-us-what-girl-power-interview-hope-evans-and-dr-katherine-mooney.

Fitzgerald, L. F., C. L. Hulin, and F. Drasgow. 1995a. "The Antecedents and Consequences of Sexual Harassment in Organizations: A Test of an Integrated Model." *Journal of Organizational Behavior* 16, (2): 123–146.

Fitzgerald, L. F., F. Drasgow, C. L. Hulin, M. J. Gelfand, and V. J. Magley. 1995b. "Antecedents and Consequences of Sexual Harassment in Organizations: A Test of an Integrated Model." *Journal of Applied Psychology* 80 (4): 557–568.

Ford-Gilboe, M., K. Jackson, T. Mantler, K. Shillington, P. Tryphonopoulos, and J. Yates. 2022. "Resilience Is More than Nature: An Exploration of the Conditions That Nurture Resilience among Rural Women Who Have Experienced IPV." *Journal of Family Violence.* https://pubmed.ncbi.nlm.nih.gov/36530539/.

Forward to Freedom. n.d. "History of the Anti Apartheid Movement." *Anti Apartheid Movement Archives.* https://www.aamarchives.org/history.html.

Foundation, S. 2023. "Women's Empowerment Programs: Fueling Resilient Communities." *Sambhav.* https://sambhavfoundation.org/blog/womens-empowerment-programs/.

Global Focus. n.d. "Community Engagement and Women's Empowerment." https://reporting.unhcr.org/global-appeal-2024/outcome-and-enabling-areas/community-engagement-and-womens-empowerment.

Gonzalez, M., L. O'Neill, and K. Statler. 2022. "Redefining Femininity: American Women in Paris in the 1920s." *Research Month*. https://digital.sandiego.edu/osp-researchweek/2022/ccurc/4/.

Hawk, T., and G. Sharkey. 2016. "What Is 'Intersectional Feminism'?" *Denison University*. https://denison.edu/academics/womens-gender-studies/feature/67969.

History.com Editors. 2009. "Women's Suffrage." *History.com*. https://www.history.com/topics/womens-history/the-fight-for-womens-suffrage.

Konrad, A. M., V. Kramer, and S. Erkut. 2010. "The Impact of Three or More Digital Identities on the Work-Life Experience of Professional Women in Europe." *Human Resource Management* 49 (1): 95–118.

Kwak, J. 2021. "Promoting Equity in the Classroom with Intersectional Pedagogy." *Every Learner Everywhere*. https://www.everylearnereverywhere.org/blog/promoting-equity-in-the-classroom-with-intersectional-pedagogy/.

Media Relations. 2022. "Systemic Gender Barriers Mean Going It Alone May Not Be the Answer for All New Women Entrepreneurs in Canada." *University of Waterloo*. https://uwaterloo.ca/news/media/systemic-gender-barriers-mean-going-it-alone-may-not-be.

Moss-Racusin, C. A., J. F. Dovidio, V. L. Brescoll, M. J. Graham, and J. Handelsman. 2012. "Science Faculty's Subtle Gender Biases Favor Male

Students." *Proceedings of the National Academy of Sciences* 109 (41): 16474–16479. https://doi.org/10.1073/pnas.1211286109.

Murphy, G. n.d. "Women's Liberation Movement." *London School of Economics and Political Science.* https://www.lse.ac.uk/library/collection-highlights/womens-liberation-movement.

Nash, J. 2016. "Gender Roles in Modern Society." *One World Education.* https://www.one-worldeducation.org/our-students-writing/gender-roles-in-modern-society/.

Ngo, Nealie Tan. 2019. "What Historical Ideals of Women's Shapes Teach Us about Women's Self-Perception and Body Decisions Today." *AMA Journal of Ethics.* https://journalofethics.ama-assn.org/article/what-historical-ideals-womens-shapes-teach-us-about-womens-self-percep-tion-and-body-decisions-today/2019-10.

Oxfam Policy and Practice. n.d. "Why Gender Matters in Activism: Feminism and Social Justice Movements." https://policy-prac-tice.oxfam.org/resources/why-gender-mat-ters-in-activism-feminism-and-social-jus-tice-movements-295481/.

Paradiso, M., L. Rollè, F. Santoniccolo, and T. Trombetta. 2023. "Gender and Media Representations: A Review of the Literature on Gender Stereotypes, Objectification and Sexualization." *International Journal of Environmental Research and Public Health.* https://www.ncbi.nlm.nih.gov/pmc/articles/PMC10218532/.

Ragins, B. R., and E. Sundstrom. 1989. "Gender and Power in Organizations: A Longitudinal Perspective." *Psychological Bulletin* 105 (1): 51–88.

The Resilient Activist. 2018. "Stories." https://www.theresilientactivist.org/stories/.

Rishi, P. 2024. "Women Freedom Fighters in India, Check Complete Details." *Physics Wallah*. https://www.pw.live/exams/ssc/women-freedom-fighters-in-india/.

Son Hing, L. and C. Stamarski. 2015. "Gender Inequalities in the Workplace: The Effects of Organizational Structures, Processes, Practices, and Decision Makers' Sexism." *Frontiers in Psychology*. https://www.frontiersin.org/journals/psychology/articles/10.3389/fpsyg.2015.01400/full.

Sorensen, R. B. 2024. "Gender and the Bible." *ResearchGate*. https://www.researchgate.net/publication/377410841_Gender_and_the_Bible.

St. Catherine University. 2022. "Gender Bias in the Workplace: Bridging the Gap." *St. Catherine University*. https://www.stkate.edu/academics/women-in-leadership-degrees/blog/gender-bias-in-the-workplace.

Steinpreis, R. E., K. A. Anders, and D. Ritzke. 1999. "The Impact of Gender on the Review of the Curricula Vitae of Job Applicants and Tenure Candidates: A National Empirical Study." *Sex Roles* 41 (7–8): 509–528. https://doi.org/10.1023/A:1018815812477.

U.S. Census Bureau. 2007. "Income, Poverty, and Health Insurance Coverage in the United States:

2006." https://www.census.gov/library/publications/2007/demo/p60-233.html.

UNESCO. 2015. "Progress on Girls' Access to Education: What the New UNESCO Data Reveals." *UNESCO.* https://www.unesco.org/en/articles/progress-girls-access-education-what-new-unesco-data-reveals.

UNESCO. 2022. "Gender Equality and Education." *UNESCO.* https://www.unesco.org/en/gender-equality/education.

United Way NCA. 2023. "Gender Roles and Gender Norms: Definition and Examples." *United Way NCA.* https://unitedwaynca.org/blog/gender-norms/.

Wilson Center. n.d. "I Belong! How Inclusion Creates a Sense of Belonging and Fuels Genuine Empowerment." *Wilson Center.* https://www.wilsoncenter.org/blog-post/i-belong-how-inclusion-creates-sense-belonging-and-fuels-genuine-empowerment.

Women On The Move Network. 2023. "Empowering through Education: The Importance of Equal Access to Learning." https://wotmnetwork.org/empowering-through-education/.

Yeshiva University. 2024. "Advancing Social Justice through Policy Change." https://online.yu.edu/wurzweiler/blog/advancing-social-justice-through-policy-change#:~:text=Yeshiva%20University's%20online%20Master%20of,social%20issues%20and%20overcome%20challenges.

About the Author

Dr. Mimi Nkwepo was born in Africa, and she went on to live in the UK as a young child. Her close family and friends fondly call her Dr. Queen Nkwepo or Dr. Queen in short because she's a force to be reckoned with. At twenty-three, she tied the knot with her husband, Dr. Eddy Nkwepo, a medical doctor and researcher by profession. They met in the USA and started a family in the suburb of Washington, DC. She's a proud mother to two awesome teenage boys who mean everything to her.

Dr. Queen is hands-on with her boys and husband, juggling it all like a pro. Putting family first is her superpower, always emphasizing the importance of balance. Many wonder how she does it all—working full-time, raising bright kids, acing at being a compassionate wife, rocking couple of businesses, and earning her doctorate—all at once. Nobody can figure out how she manages her busy schedule, family life, career, and entrepreneurial ventures although she is exemplary of a true role model for girls and women today. Dr. Mommy, as some call her, radiates positivity. She's all about finding light in the dark, spreading good vibes, and encouraging others to do the same.

Dr. Queen is a shining example of optimism who inspires young adults, especially girls, with her passion for women's empowerment.

Always with a smile, she is known for her contagious joy and readiness to lend a hand. Dancing, working out, and living life to the max are what motivate her. Intentional and focused on her professional life, she kicked off her career in hospitality management and later transitioned to human resources and talent acquisition after her second son was born. Fueling her love for helping others, Dr. Mimi Nkwepo pursued a master's in human resource management and a doctor of business administration in HR management from Thomas Edison State University.

Dr. Mimi Nkwepo is currently rocking it as the National Head of Talent Acquisition at Coach USA, and she also chairs the Thomas Edison State University School of Management Dean's advisory board. She is passionate about embracing and celebrating African culture and heritage, and she volunteers her service to various causes to support kids back in Africa.